The
Snowflake
Effect

Trey Willis

To Dad for always reminding me that I wasn't special.

And to Nana for always reminding me that I was.

And to Cousin Jarod of House Fornes for offering notes, and encouragement from beginning to bitter end.

And to Gretchen for happily tolerating all of my various schemes and shenanigans and being an all-around better wife than I deserve.

And also Mom, because she would never forgive me for thanking all these other people and leaving her out.

"You are not special. You're not a beautiful and unique snowflake. You're the same decaying organic matter as everything else. We're all part of the same compost heap."

Chuck Palahniuk, Fight Club

"The Self-Esteem Movement revolved around a single notion, the idea that every child is special. Boy, they said it over and over and over, as if to remind themselves. Every child is special. And I kept saying fuck you; every child is clearly not special."

George Carlin

CONTENTS

PROLOGUE

There was a precise moment in time where it all fell apart and everything went to hell. That moment was at a little league baseball game, of all things. It was the instant that the first pitch was released at the first game where no score would be kept. I have no way of knowing the specifics of when and where this occurred, even though I have my suspicions regarding both. When and where it happened are much less important than the fact *that* it happened. With the release of that pitch, we invested fully in the idea that high self-esteem was the most important thing we could give children.

During that game, probably around the top of the third inning, snow began to drift downward, a flurry at first. 'How beautiful' we thought, 'every flake is a unique and beautiful gift.' Someone almost certainly pointed out that Eskimos have many different words for snow in a condescending tone suggesting that nobody else is aware of this, despite the fact that someone *always* mentions this when it snows. There we stood, gawking upward at the falling snow. None of us noticed the dark clouds accumulating on the horizon.

The flakes became larger, but no less special or unique. Exponentially more began to tumble downward, pushing and shoving each other out of the way, fighting for the validation and admiration to which they felt so entitled. Thunder grumbled all around, preventing us from denying the inherent beauty of each flake. Lighting ripped through the sky, burning away all sense of rationality or responsibility. Snowstorms with thunder and lightning are a factual sign of impending doom, by the way. Trophy sized hail crashed down, at least one for each of us.

Before we could grasp the reality of what was happening, we were stumbling snow-blind through the whiteout. Desperately we clawed our way forward, searching for some beacon of hope. The wind howled around us, preventing cries of warning or sensibility from being heard by those who would be spared if only they could see and hear what was taking place just out of sight. Soon the snow packed into our mouths and stopped even the most futile of whimpers from being audible, even to ourselves. We all froze to death on that field, together and alone, covered by millions of flakes, all of unquestionable and unwavering specialness.

For nearly thirty years, the snows have fallen without reprieve. The flurries that began in the 1980s are long gone, only lasting long enough to distract us from the coming storm. Everything that our culture had been prior to the onset of the Self-Esteem Movement disappeared beneath the drifts. Our values and norms suffocated in the crushing white silence long ago; only the snow remains.

Winter is coming.

Nope.

Now is the winter of my discontent.

Not that either.

Shit.

I can't think of anything witty or dramatic to say.

I was born in 1985, which realistically makes me too young to write a book on this subject. However, it also gives me, and those of my generation, a unique perspective on the current state of our culture. Who better to write a war story than someone who had their boots on the ground, I say. While many other people have addressed the subject of self-esteem and how its movement has negatively impacted my generation, they have generally complained about *us* from without. I, on the other hand, will be complaining about *everything*, and doing so from within. This internal perspective, in my mind, lends much credibility to my argument.

Sociologists, psychologists, the media, educators and members of older generations have called us by many different names. Generation Me. The Facebook Generation. The Internet Generation. The iGeneration. The Millennials. The Trophy Kids. The Snowflake Children. Given the context in which my generation is usually discussed, it's not surprising that many of these names are accompanied by negative connotations.

Despite the variety of names at our disposal, I still prefer the original of my generation – Generation Y. It's not creative, and it says nothing relevant about us aside from the fact that we have done little to earn a better name for ourselves. We aren't cool enough to be Generation X, but we came of age riding their grungy, nihilistic coattails. We aren't special at all, and could have easily been another Lost Generation, floundering with no real purpose, except that someone decided that we should all be special, or at least believe we were.

We were the last group of people to be born still able to remember what our society was like prior to the internet. We were also the first group of people to become hopelessly reliant on the internet, the irony of which is not lost on us. We will do nothing great or noteworthy as a generation. If we are discussed in the future at all, the conversation will involve the internet, and how awful and selfish we were.

For the duration of this book, I will periodically mention other generations. For the sake of clarity, these are the name and approximate range of birth years that I associate with each of them.

- Greatest Generation – 1910-1930
- The Lost Generation – 1931-1945
- The Baby Boomers – 1946-1964
- Generation X – 1965-1982
- Generation Y – 1983-1995
- Millennials – 1996-2008

These are generally agreed upon with one exception – I separate Generation Y and Millennials into two groups. I feel that generational cohorts are becoming smaller because the speed of societal development is ever increasing, resulting in groups of people who have fundamentally different experiences with increasing frequency. In reality, this is a personal choice and has little bearing on my argument since the negative aspects discussed generally hold true for both generations.

Throughout the late 1980s and 1990s, American culture put fierce and unyielding emphasis on building, fostering, and reinforcing the highest self-esteem in its children. In most cases, this is referred to as the Self-Esteem Movement. Looking back, this shift in values holds at least partial accountability for many of the negative qualities evident in our society.

Self-esteem seemed like a good idea at the time, and truthfully, it was a good idea. However, as we all (should) know, a good idea does not necessary guarantee positive results. The Self-Esteem Movement is, and has continued to be, a colossal failure. It has failed me, my generation, and our entire culture in a staggering number of ways.

As a society we have changed, and generally not for the better. Becoming a culture where we have made it a top priority to create children with highest self-esteem possible at all costs is at the crux of many of our cultural ills. The collateral damage from this type of thinking is immeasurable. We became so fixated on creating confident children that we ignored many of the negative repercussions this idea was causing.

We are a horribly deluded and selfish generation of people. We feel entitled to success, despite our overall disinterest in working toward our goals. We are special, and unique, and intelligent, and better than everyone else. This mentality didn't spring from the cultural ether unprovoked. A perfect storm of changing societal norms, values, laziness, and good intentions molded us into the hollow, self-worshipping animals we have become.

What follows is based on nothing more than my own cultural outlook, opinions, observations, research and pervasive cynicism. Some of these I have made independently, and some are derived from ideas and observations shared with me by those who have been kind enough to discuss this subject with me. My points will be sarcastic and hyperbolic more often than not, but the issue itself is all too real, and desperately needs to be addressed.

From here, I will mount my high horse and proceed to ride it into the sunset of this book. Once the horse is dead, I will beat it time and time again.

You have been warned.

You are not special. Neither am I. The sooner we can all agree upon, and embrace this simple truth, the happier we will all be.

EVERYONE GETS A TROPHY

At some point in my adolescence, everyone was getting trophies all the time for almost any reason at all. For a while, nobody was even keeping score at little league games. Everyone was a winner. Presently, youth basketball leagues in my town will stop increasing the score of the winning team after a certain margin. I can only assume the same is true in other places as well.

This was not something that occurred when I was playing little league. Something about this seemed fundamentally wrong to me. I was awful at baseball, and forced to recognize and accept this. My peers, coaches, parents, and overall lack of success in the sport ensured that I was aware of my shortcomings, which is in no way a negative thing.

The only time I can remember being anything less than terrible at baseball was one of the first seasons where the kids pitch. I was probably around ten years old. This was not anything of my own doing, but a function of my size – I was such a small kid that I generally got walked. Because of this, I felt pretty good knowing that I couldn't ruin too much for my team playing right field, and could pretty much guarantee an on base each time I stepped to the plate. I genuinely enjoyed playing baseball that season. We won third place that year, out of probably eight or nine teams, which still stands as my highest achievement in sport.

Quickly after that season, kids became faster, pitchers became more accurate, and the athletic separated themselves from the un-athletic. The last season I played I was fourteen. I had one on base, zero hits, and completely missed the only ball that came my way in right field. Clearly, baseball was no longer for me.

This memory is valuable to me. Had I been born a part of any other generation, it would be an arbitrary memory of my youth, hardly worth the effort to recall. Because I was born into a generation that was subjected to the Self-Esteem Movement, it is a significant and defining experience. I was allowed to be bad at baseball just before it was no longer acceptable to allow children to be bad at things.

I was not handed a trophy and told I was great at baseball. It was never implied that I could play pro ball, or even in high school. I was told (not cruelly) that I just wasn't good enough at baseball to play on a competitive level. It occurred to me at that point that I had no real interest in putting in the time and effort to become a better baseball player, so I devoted my time, attention, and energy to other pursuits.

I was taught to accept this as a constructive force and to use that information to inform my decisions in a positive way. It reaffirmed the fundamental value that my parents had worked my entire childhood to instill in me – if you want something badly enough, you will work for it. The truth was I didn't want it badly enough, and I wouldn't work for it; so I chose to not play baseball. My ego was not destroyed. My world view did not collapse. The information was presented to me at face value, which allowed me process it and move forward in life with increased self-awareness.

Because the areas in which I excelled were reinforced and areas where I lacked were not, I was able to develop an actual and authentic personal identity. Had I been told that I was great at baseball, or any number of other things (usually involving running, throwing, or competitiveness) and internalized these messages, my identity would almost certainly have become muddled and frustrating.

Let's take this to an extreme for the sake of amusement. In this hypothetical scenario everything is the same – I am just as bad at baseball as I truly was (and still am, I suppose). The only difference is that society had chosen to eliminate many of the factors that would point this out in an obvious way – score is not kept at games, everyone has to play an equal amount of time, everyone gets a trophy at the end of the season, there are no all-star games, my parents (and/or other significant adult figures) are encouraged to tell me how great I am at baseball, the list could (and seemingly does) go on forever.

What if I internalized this and believed that I was actually an amazing baseball player? What if it became a vital part of my self-identity? Any of these outcomes suggest a person who lacks self-awareness and is basing their identity on external factors. Without an understanding of oneself, it is hard to accurately identify positive qualities and pursue activities in which one will be successful. If this is the case, then I would very easily find myself acquainted with frequent and bitter disappointment as an adult after realizing that these things were not true. Reassessing your whole identity after one of the cornerstones has been ripped out is not a quick and painless task, and could be the beginnings of a pretty serious crisis of identity.

By reinforcing things that aren't true you are setting up a child for some degree of emotional difficulty in the future. It's unintentionally selfish on the part of the parent/adult who benefits by not inflicting any potential or perceived pain on the child. The uncomfortable truth is that you are doing your child a tremendous disservice by 'protecting' them and almost certainly guaranteeing a more significant degree of pain in your child's future.

I grew up with a guy that this happened to, and have witnessed first-hand just how devastating it can be. All throughout our childhood he was a dominate athlete. He excelled at any sport he cared to participate in, and was always involved in baseball, football, or basketball. In high school, he was well-regarded in all three sports, but was especially adept at basketball. I imagine he would have been an excellent lacrosse player as well, had it existed in our one-horse town.

Growing up in a small town is important in this story because it strongly factors into his ability to be (and to be perceived as) a dominant athlete. He was one of the best basketball players he had ever met; he just hadn't met that many people. His parents were not overly indulgent and did not exaggerate his abilities. They actively encouraged his involvement in sports and always pushed him to be the best at whatever he did. He was praised when he did well, and critiqued when he performed poorly. Even without intentionally baseless reinforcement from his parents, he still internalized the belief that he was an amazing basketball player.

Being North Carolinian ensures a few things, one of which is that you are morally obligated to care about college basketball, at least a little. The sum of his aspirations was to play basketball for the University of North Carolina at Chapel Hill. He was single minded in this goal, and nothing else would suffice. The primary aspect of his identity was being a basketball player who was good enough to play for one of the best collegiate basketball programs in the country. Interestingly enough, he never talked about dreams of playing in the NBA, just Chapel Hill. This in itself is telling, because it implies that he felt like playing basketball at Chapel Hill was a realistic and obtainable goal.

Ultimately, he was not accepted into Chapel Hill, despite being an above average student. He attended North Carolina State University that fall and established a short-term goal of walking on to their basketball team with intentions of transferring to Chapel Hill, where he would achieve his primary goal. I was never sure if he was given the opportunity to try out for the basketball team at State, but I know that he never played there.

He sank into depression and dropped out of school before his second semester was over. That spring, he moved back to our hometown, and it took him quite some time to recover from the fact that he was unable to obtain the only thing he ever wanted. The thing that he *knew to be true* because it had been unintentionally reinforced by environmental factors was no longer true. This is enough to break most people. Imagine how much worse this might have been had he also been nursed on the false assurance of the Self-Esteem Movement.

This will be an unpopular statement: it is not fair to the winners to stop keeping score and give everyone a trophy. They say winning isn't everything, and they are right, but it is *something*, and it's also important for a litany of reasons. We need to learn how to lose, and to lose with dignity. Just as importantly, we need to know what winning feels like, and learn how to win gracefully. These translate into essential, real world skills later in life. We are robbing our children of vital experiences for their social development by discouraging the concept of winners and losers.

Learning to win with grace helps us do things like appropriately manage a promotion, especially when your peers (who may have applied for the same promotion) become your subordinates. A person who has never learned to win with dignity could easily handle the situation badly and end up with a staff that does not respect him/her. Gloating or talking down to former peers is a proven way to create a staff that will undermine and defy you with regularity.

The opposite of this scenario is also true. If we are never allowed to lose, we are not equipped to effectively navigate the disappointment of being passed over for a promotion. We are not capable of being genuinely happy for our peer because we never learned how to properly express that feeling. Instead, we may choose to pout or harbor resentment in some other adult fashion, quite possibly being fired because of our decreased productivity and our newly developed negative attitude.

We owe it to ourselves and our society to give the experience of winning and losing to our children. It is such a fundamental experience for a child to know the intense joy of winning as well as the bitter sadness of defeat. Winning, and losing for that matter, encourage the development of socially desirable traits in human beings. These include, but certainly are not limited to, reinforcing the value of hard work and dedication, sportsmanship (which we call respect and common decency in every other setting), humility, and increased feelings of self-worth.

As a child, winning feels better than almost anything imaginable. Its ability to reinforce and demand repetition is not unlike that of a drug. Wanting to obtain that feeling again will actively encourage hard work in order to increase performance, therefore increasing the chances you will win (and feel good) again. It's not hard to see where I am going with this.

If the feeling of winning encourages good work ethic in a child playing a game, then he or she will internalize the value of working for their achievements in the future. This may mean working diligently to secure a promotion or raise. I suppose it could also mean putting in long hours of research and physical preparation to become the best burglar of all time, but generally speaking, a strong work ethic is a good thing. Losing actually reinforces this as well. If you understand how good it feels to win, and truly care about whatever game you are playing, then the idea of working to improve in order to achieve victory is reinforced.

As children we are universally told that it is good to be a 'good winner' and bad to be a 'sore loser.' This relates to the concept of sportsmanship, being respectful to others in the game. We are taught to congratulate the winners after losing, and to enjoy winning without being arrogant or otherwise shoving it in the face of the losers.

Respect is a fundamental value in our society. This is true across all settings, and by reinforcing the idea of social prudence through sportsmanship, children are encouraged to be more respectful as adults. The advantages of this are numerous and obvious and don't need to be listed out individually. Suffice it to say, people who are 'good sports' are usually viewed more positively by others both socially and professionally.

Hubris. I use this word to an obnoxious degree, especially when I am mostly certain that my present company does not know the meaning or origin of the word (which isn't unembarrassing to admit, and also a shitty thing to do). Hubris is a Greek concept suggesting that the gods punish those who act without humility. To act with arrogance is punishable. This idea is reiterated in countless different ways across countless different cultures. The meek shall inherit the earth is another notable instance of this same basic concept – to act with humility is something that should be rewarded.

Winning and losing help foster the socially desirable trait of humility. We compliment the losing team when we win. We are expected to congratulate the winning team when we lose. It was (and hopefully still is) abhorrent behavior to gloat about winning to the loser. Nobody likes arrogance even though confidence is a desirable trait to many. Winning, losing, and the concept of sportsmanship help to define the difference.

Giving everyone a trophy and never acknowledging that there are winners and losers in all things is a (seemingly) noble concept that has its foundation firmly planted in the idea that it helps foster high self-esteem in all children. This is an overly simple idea at best. Obviously, winning can, and does, create high self-esteem. No reasonable person would argue otherwise. What I contend is that losing can also help to develop a positive self-concept and result in high self-esteem.

Losing is frustrating and awful, especially as a child when whatever game you happen to be playing is just about the most important endeavor you have ever engaged in. We want to win because losing sucks. In order to win we have to work hard and commit to achieving a goal.

Learning to be a good sport, especially after a loss, helps us relate to our peers in socially appropriate ways as an adult. This increased ability to communicate effectively leads to a higher number of positive interactions with others both socially and professionally. Those with good communication skills are more successful in their careers. They are usually easily likeable people. This is a recipe for increased feelings of self-worth and self-esteem. If others like me, then I must be likeable, ergo I like myself. Losing with dignity as a child reinforces the development and internalization of these vital communication skills.

Another, probably less likely, scenario in which being allowed to lose increases self-esteem is something I have observed in my own experience. As I have already mentioned, I was terrible at baseball, and most other athletic things. Because I was allowed to experience this, and accept it as truth, I was able to divert my attention to things that I ultimately ended up enjoying far more than sports. By being allowed to lose, I was given the opportunity to seek out activities where I excel.

Had I continued playing sports (badly) past childhood I may never have discovered that I am musically talented. I wouldn't play piano or guitar, both of which I continue to enjoy as an adult. Music brings me satisfaction. Being adept at playing music is equally satisfying. Objectively, my self-esteem is higher because I am a musician. Losing at baseball allowed me to explore and 'win' at things like music.

Lastly, but not unimportantly, there is the issue

that eliminating winners and losers takes away from the experience of being a child itself. Despite the ways in which winning and losing help to prepare children for adulthood, winning is something that every person should experience. I would gladly lose nine times to win on the tenth. So would you. And so would your kids. This is, and will always be, infinitely preferable to having no chance of winning at all.

Shoving a trophy into the hands of every child does nothing but cause problems for them in the end. It clouds their ability to accurately perceive themselves and develop any sort of realistic self-awareness. They are stripped of the opportunity to learn about their strengths and weaknesses and are ill equipped to receive criticism as an adult. When everyone gets a trophy, it becomes hard to know who actually deserved one in the first place. If everyone is a winner, and everyone is special, is *anyone* special? The answer, in case you are wondering: not really.

SPECIAL LITTLE SNOWFLAKES

I have been a therapist for a number of years, and in that time, I have come to only two definitive conclusions. The first is that the positive relationship I develop with my clients is far more important than any skills I employ in session. The second is that we are not unique. We may have some idiosyncratic qualities, but we are not unique. I am regularly confronted with this reality due to how quickly I can accurately infer things about a person after gathering a relatively small amount of demographic information related to their current and past life circumstances.

We are not special, unique little snowflakes. We are merely one of many people who are very similar to each other. This is not to say that everyone is the same. There are types of people, and those types have a high degree of variance. Within those groups, there are people who have unique qualities, but this does not make them unique. If we must observe small and inconsequential details of a person to find uniqueness, then they are not unique. This is in no way a bad thing, but telling children they are completely unique and special, implies that it is a potentially bad thing to be like other people, and *that* is a bad thing.

I've had some (relatively) unique experiences in my life. For instance, in a three-month period of time when I was twenty-two, I was diagnosed with cancer and stood next to my father's hospital bed while he took his dying breath. I seriously doubt that there are more than a few people in the world who have experienced that particular set of circumstances in exactly the same way. This does not make me unique. It makes me a person who had cancer, and a person whose father died at a young age. Neither of these are unique situations, millions of people can relate to one or both experiences.

Like every other person walking the earth, I fit nicely into categories. I meet people like me all the time. They can easily relate to me because of our shared lack of uniqueness. We usually call these people our friends. It would be unadulterated chaos if each of us actually were unique – nobody could really understand, or relate to anyone else. Human socialization and friendship is built upon shared experience and commonality. A six-year-old isn't exactly equipped with the cognitive fortitude necessary to integrate the conflicting ideas that they are utterly unique while simultaneously being taught that friendship is based on similarity.

Not surprisingly, this concept was popularized by the Self-Esteem Movement in the eighties and nineties. Also not surprisingly, it was a short sighted and terrible idea. Again we have a situation where parents and/or other adults are allegedly protecting children from experiencing pain by ensuring that the child knows that they are completely unique, special, and one of a kind. This is supposed to encourage the child to develop high self-esteem, which is not a bad thing; but the *way* it encourages high self-esteem is a bad thing.

Despite the fact that it's just not true, constantly reinforcing the ideas of uniqueness and specialness in the same concept is potentially harmful. A child could easily internalize the idea that they must be different in order to be special. Add into this equation that adults are telling *groups* of children that they are all special and unique and it's not hard to see how this could become confusing very quickly. Their self-esteem could be damaged simply because children are capable of recognizing the fact that they are similar to their friends. If they are like their friends, then the assumption is they are not unique, which means they are not special. If everybody is special then nobody is special.

Fostering the idea of uniqueness and specialness during childhood can (somewhat predictably) invite significant decreases in self-esteem as an adult. Your employer probably doesn't think you are a unique and inherently special person. Neither does your landlord. Or your mortgage company. Or almost anybody who isn't your mother, except maybe your grandmother.

Telling children they are special in an ambiguous way heavily contributes to the entitlement that exists in younger generations. If I am special then I obviously deserve special treatment. A person of specialness should not have to start in an entry level position. A person who is knowingly special does not have to ascribe to the rules if they feel justified in breaking them. A special person is overqualified and refuses to do work that is obviously beneath their level of specialness. A person, having obtained a certain level of specialness, deserves corner offices, frequent promotions, and annual bonuses. As a therapist, but especially as a person, these are alarmingly narcissistic behaviors.

In addition to being a therapist, I have also been known to moonlight as a psychology professor for a community college. Courses I taught were online, which I concede accounts for some of the brazen arrogance of the following interactions, but it simply cannot explain them all. My teaching experience has made it abundantly clear that younger people are no longer interested in taking responsibility for their own actions, especially when there are negative consequences associated with those actions.

I maintain a late work policy that is more than fair – I will accept late work if legitimate circumstances prevent you from completing the assignment on time, and/or you contact me prior to the due date to arrange terms for late submission. Despite this, every semester I receive at least one email from students who have failed to complete the vast majority of the assignments asking to turn in all of their work in the last week of the course. Inevitably, when asked why they did not complete the work as assigned nor had any communication with me during the semester, the response is usually something like "I just blew off the class, but now I'm ready to do the work because I don't want to fail." Another favorite of mine are students who will attempt to submit an assignment a week or more after the due date with an explanation about "being busy the day the assignment was due," or the ever popular "I know you don't accept late work, but was hoping you would still accept this."

When I have refused these assignments I've been called unfair, asked for my supervisor's information, and had complaints made against me. Once, a student even told me that his grade was too low because I wouldn't accept his late work. The students have internalized the idea that I am obligated to make exceptions for them. I am supposed to accept their work because they are special and deserve preferential treatment. The events that prevented them from completing their assignments constitute legitimate circumstances in their minds, including laziness and irresponsibility. The part I find the most frustrating is that the blame is not entirely theirs. Had these people not been aggressively told they were special and unique, the majority of them would not behave in this way.

The more insidious factor lurking just out of sight is the vagueness with which children are told they are special. It's so insincere that some children actually realize how ridiculous the whole thing is. I am in no way suggesting that we should tell our children they are not special. That would be absurd. What I am suggesting is that we stop telling children they are ambiguously special. Everyone is special in some way, but no one is so blindingly special that it permeates every facet of their existence. If our end game as a society is to generate honest, authentic, respectful, and productive people, we should start by being honest, authentic, and respectful in our interactions with children.

Telling a child they are special in a prepackaged, generic way does more harm than good. It generates people who assume many things are beneath them, that the rules do not apply to them in any conventional sense, and are entitled to much more than they actually are. Be specific. If a child is special because they have an uncanny ability to learn new languages, then tell them that's what makes them special. If you are exceptionally good at building or repairing engines, then you are special in that regard. If you draw well, excel at math, tell stories well, are physically attractive, athletic, cook well, play the accordion, write sonnets, compose music – no matter what it is, the things you do objectively better than the general population are what make you special. It takes very little time and energy to identify one of these qualities, yet we continue to travel the low road because expending even the slightest effort is immeasurably more difficult than no effort at all.

I realize that this seems to work against my argument that you, your children, and everyone you know are not special, which is true to some degree. However, the harm is not that we are told we are special; it is *how* and *to what degree* we are told we are special. I'm special because I am intelligent and gifted with music. You are special for whatever reason it is that makes you special. Neither of us is special enough to warrant any more or any less and any other person out there. Being totally and all encompassingly special means that I am totally entitled to totally have everything that I want, and I totally don't have to work for it. I am assuming you can totally see the difference between these two concepts. If not, then your ability to reason is probably not what makes you special.

Let's all just go ahead and agree that kids can't be whatever they want to be. This is completely false, and we should probably stop saying it entirely. It's one of the most dishonest things we tell children. The child who is failing sixth grade math has just about zero chance of becoming an astronaut. The child who can't compete in little league will not be starting short stop for the Atlanta Braves. The boy who has failed high school biology twice won't be a doctor. The girl with severe asthma isn't on track to be an Olympic sprinter.

When children think about their ambitions and future, their thoughts are usually completely untethered from reality. They just want to be a lawyer and (insert trusted adult figure here) has told them they can be whatever they want to be. Without a fully developed prefrontal cortex, children (and many adolescents) lack the capacity to understand that their ability to excel in particular tasks directly impacts their ability to achieve their goals. In this instance, the child may not realize that his or her traditionally poor academic performance is a pretty strong indicator that they will not be able to pass the LSAT or get into law school.

Children are unrealistic by nature, which is one

of the primary reasons that being a child is completely amazing. Well, that, and the total lack of responsibility. As parents, adults, and caretakers, it is our duty to introduce and foster realism in children as they age. If we never learn to be rational as a child, we will likely have significant difficulty developing this very necessary skill as an adult. Like reading, or any number of other things generally learned in childhood, it is much easier to learn how to think realistically as a child than to undo a lifetime of delusion as an adult.

If a person internalizes the idea that they can be anything they want to be, then that person will end up disappointed with their life as an adult. This is another example of efforts to increase self-esteem in children likely having an inverse effect in the long term. For their entire life, children have been led to believe they could be (insert irrational aspiration here). Once they reach adulthood, this certainty is challenged and there is nothing left to reinforce it. Their self-esteem will suffer because of this and they will be supremely disap-pointed. If we collectively decide to be honest with our children, we can prevent this from happening.

It goes beyond that, though. If we are honest with our children and help them to establish realistic expec-tations, not only will they avert disappointment, but also increase self-esteem by setting goals that they can, and will achieve. Say your child wants to be a doctor. Instead of offering blind assurance, have an honest conversation with the child about what it takes to meet that goal. When they are young, this is as simple as telling them that doctors have to be very intelligent and go to school for a long time, which means that they need to really focus and do well in school.

As they get older, you can discuss the importance of doing well in science courses since Pre-Med programs put a lot of focus on biology and anatomy courses. Once they have transitioned to college, remind them how hard it actually is to get into Medical school and how too much partying and low grades during their freshmen year is enough to ruin their chances. By being honest with your child and offering realistic guidance, you actually increase the chances that they will succeed.

I'm not advocating for people to crush the dreams of their children. Maybe putting a dent in them here and there isn't such a bad idea, though. Unrealistic expectations should not be actively encouraged because they will often result in falling short of the mark. Shooting for the moon and missing doesn't mean that you land among the stars. It means that you suffocate or freeze to death in the desolation of space.

We are an achievement driven culture. However, actually accomplishing something and being told we can accomplish anything are not the same thing, and do not provide the same sort of increase in feelings of self-worth. Foster realistic goals, even if they are not overly ambitious, and watch the happiness and satisfaction that occurs when they are achieved.

WORKING FOR THE WEEKEND

When did showing up to work on time, rarely leaving early, and going only slightly above your stated job duties become synonymous with phenomenal work ethic? Take a minute and really consider that. Maybe I only have this perception because I have lived my entire life in the South, where things happen at a generally slower pace than the rest of the country. Maybe it has something to do with my penchant for living in beach towns, where things can be slower still. Maybe I am the only one with this perception, but somehow I doubt it. People, especially younger people, are astonishingly lazy.

I have been told that I have a strong work ethic on more than one occasion by more than one employer. There is no other way for me to write that sentence without it being even more embarrassing and self-righteous than it already is. Either way, it had to be done to illustrate the rest of my point. I have never believed this because I don't actually have an uncanny work ethic – it just seems that way when compared to other members of my generation.

Showing up and doing your job is literally the bare minimum an employer can ask of you. I have done a bit more than this and been considered a model employee.

41

Fortunately for society, this is not something unique to me, quite a few members of my generation appear to be capitalizing on this and establishing themselves in their chosen careers. Unfortunately, we appear to be an overwhelming minority.

I sincerely appreciate the fact that my slightly above average approach to work is often viewed as mind blowing dedication and drive. It has made my early adulthood relatively easy. I sometimes selfishly hope that it stays this way and I continue to reap the rewards of my outstanding work by comparison. When I stop being selfish, I realize that this gleeful and willing underperformance is a real problem, and it has to stop.

If you guessed the Self-Esteem Movement was somehow to blame for this, then you have obviously been paying attention.

Entitlement is a word traditionally reserved for the middle and upper tiers of society to talk down about people of lower socioeconomic status who receive any kind of government assistance or benefit. It still serves that same purpose, but now it has another prominent meaning as well. Entitlement is often used to describe younger people who feel like things are owed to them in some fashion.

In its modern connotation, entitlement may refer to the sixteen-year-old girl that cries when she does not receive a new car on her birthday. It may be used to describe the twenty-something that feels like being hired at anything less than $50,000 a year is not worth his time or effort. I have frequently used this term to describe students who feel that they should be allowed to ignore due dates and submit assignments on their own time frame. I assume that three examples are more than sufficient for you to get the point.

The irony in all of this is in the identity of the people who are so freely throwing around that particular descriptor. They are the same people who have been arbitrarily telling children that they are special and unique and can be anything they want to be if they just want it enough. They are the same people *guaranteeing* that these children will be successful, and only some-times with the caveat of 'as long as you go to college.' By selfishly refusing to impart realism in their children, they have created a generation of people who have such recklessly high self-esteem that they believe they are objectively more deserving than others are.

Nobody talks about how absurd this actually is. The parents and adults responsible for shaping my generation are allowed to avoid the responsibility of creating responsible people *and* get to bitch about all the negative qualities that have come about in younger adults as a direct result of this. That is the equivalent of setting your house on fire, then bemoaning your terrible luck because your house just burned to the ground.

By reinforcing self-esteem without regard, we have created a culture of entitlement. This was initially confined to Generation Y, but has since permeated other generations as well. Not surprisingly, this is most easily observed in members of younger generations. It is not uncommon to hear anyone over twenty lamenting about the level of brazen entitlement that is displayed in 'kids these days.' This is something that is easily observed, and just as easily commented upon.

Every week or two there is a news story about Generation Y or the Millennials (which are lumped together more often than not). These stories are all the same – some newscaster or guest talks about how the current generation is selfish and entitled and lazy. They sometimes go as far as identifying factors that have contributed to this, which are usually some combination of the internet, Facebook, cell phones, and the economy. None attempt to discuss solutions or ways to prevent future generations from similar outcomes. Nobody bothers to talk solutions because the problem is so insidious and interwoven into our value system that discussing solutions forces us reassess every facet ourselves, both culturally and individually, which is a tremendously uncomfortable undertaking.

The seeds of this whole debacle were sown when the parents, teachers, and other allegedly responsible adult figures started aggressively fueling self-esteem in the late eighties. I am not suggesting that all parents are guilty of this, especially when it first began. However, enough of them embraced this idea that it created a significant number of children with obscene levels of self-esteem and a sense of entitlement. Over time, a war of attrition began. Parents and adults who did not initially buy into the Self-Esteem Movement slowly began to crumble under the mounting cultural pressure.

As a society, we placed ever increasing value on fostering self-esteem in our children with the hope of creating successful and confident adults. Obviously, this is a great idea, despite its horribly misguided implementation. What this value eventually became is a cultural norm more akin to "you don't love your children as much as everyone else if you don't ensure they have high self-esteem." Even worse, it could just as easily be interpreted as "if your child does not have high self-esteem, you have failed as a parent."

America is a very material culture, even though we sometimes try to pretend it isn't. Success and worth can be measured with possessions. Self-worth and net worth are essentially interchangeable terms. It was no longer enough to tell your children they are special, you have to *show* them how special they are.

In order to maintain a viable level of self-esteem we must shower our children and ourselves with the newest and best of everything. They may no longer feel adequate if they don't have the newest cell phones, or gaming consoles, or a nice car to wreck when they turn sixteen. Value must be demonstrated in tangible ways; otherwise, they cannot prove to others how special they are. If they are unable to outwardly present their worth, their self-esteem may decrease.

Reaffirming their child's self-esteem at this point would take a good deal of time and frustrating work. To solve this problem, parents are forced to choose between reckless consumerism, and putting in some serious time wrestling with the entitlement that has spread like a cancer through our society. Welcome to America where throwing money at a problem is usually the first and correct decision.

Another aspect of the Self-Esteem Movement that has proven to be detrimental in the long term is the flippant assurance of upward mobility. Obviously, this is not a new concept within our culture; the 'American Dream' is often quantified as the possibility of upward mobility. However, as a culture, we have started promising that upward mobility is a certainty. We are telling children that they are special to such a degree that they believe they are better than other people and entitled to more than everyone else. And then we are guaranteeing upward mobility.

Children and adolescents will undoubtedly have increased feelings of self-worth when told they are special, and will be successful without regard to anything factual. No one bothered to consider the ramifications of these actions once these adolescents reach adulthood only to find that upward mobility is far from a certainty, and that they are not actually that special. Success is no longer a guarantee. You might not be as special as you know you are. The realities of adult life are no longer congruent with the truths of childhood.

The resulting identity confusion can give way to disappointment, depression, defeat, despair, disillusion, and probably even more words that start with the letter 'D.' Regardless of what letter the words start with, they are all consistent with an adult who has lower self-esteem because his or her world view has been challenged in a way that they realistically cannot deny. That person is forced to consider the validity of *all* the truths in his or her life. Reassessing your entire belief system causes significant duress for essentially anyone.

I imagine (or at least hope) that this promise of upward mobility has started to slow, and will have a far smaller negative impact on future generations than it did on my own. Many members of my generation were the product of households in which one, or both parents did not attend college. This is likely the genesis of the link between self-esteem and upward mobility.

My parents are guilty of this. For the majority of my childhood I was pushed to excel in school because the expectation was that I would go to college. I was told constantly that I would be successful as long as I had a college degree. Most of my peers were inoculated with this idea as well, and most of us zealously believed it. This was at least somewhat true at the time, but like most things related the Self-Esteem Movement, nobody bothered to consider the long term implications.

Imagine my disappointment when I opted to pursue a degree in psychology. Upon the realization that I would be borderline unemployable with this degree, I decided to attend graduate school for counseling, which is employable but also guarantees almost no possibility of upward mobility. I admit that my starting salary left me more than a little disheartened with the world and the real value of an education.

Obviously, my parents meant well, and used the promise of upward mobility as motivation to ensure that

I obtained education beyond what they had at the time. I do not fault them for this – it never occurred to them how useless a psychology degree actually is, they were just happy I hadn't chosen to study music. However, I sometimes have nagging feelings about what my life would have been like had I decided to pursue a degree that had more viable career options associated with it. A blow was dealt to my self-esteem because I had internalized an unrealistic expectation to be more successful than my family of origin because I got a degree.

Only 27% of bachelor's level college graduates work in a field that directly corresponds to their chosen major. Census data from 2010 shows that 62% of college graduates find employment requiring a degree, meaning that approximately 35% of college graduates work in a field unrelated to their degree. The remaining 38% are unable to find employment equivalent to their education at all. These are disheartening numbers to anyone currently amassing, or chipping away at, mountains of student loan debt.

In 2010, 48% of college graduates were working jobs requiring less than a bachelor's degree. More alarmingly, 38% of these graduates were employed in jobs requiring less than a high school diploma. Many people who have been told they were special, and guaranteed success once they finished their education framed their degrees only to continue waiting tables, tending bar, or working retail. The juxtaposition between their reality and the values forced upon them by the Self-Esteem Movement has to be maddening. A person of factual specialness could never fall so short of their goal. By promising their children upward mobility, success, and bolstering self-esteem without regard to the future, parents and caregivers reap short-term rewards while sowing complex, long-term failure for their children.

Underemployment is not a problem that is likely to diminish in the near future. Projections indicate that 19 million people will obtain bachelor's degrees from 2010-2020, while employment requiring a bachelor's degree will grow by only 7 million. There will be fierce competition for these positions, which will almost certainly be underpaid by companies that realize how valuable their jobs actually are.

This is the best case scenario we can offer our hopeful college graduates – overworked, underpaid, and unappreciated because your employer knows just how easily you can be replaced. The 12 million new degree holders who aren't fortunate enough to land one of these jobs will be serving food, making coffee, and selling televisions. Most of them will be unable to reconcile their level of self-esteem and entitlement with the reality of their job at Trader Joe's or Best Buy. This fuels the diminished work ethic seen in young people, especially those who are underemployed. Whether that underemployment is factual or a manifestation of their inflated self-worth is another matter entirely.

Adolescents with unrealistic levels of self-esteem are being protected from reality and will suffer because of their lack of preparedness for the real world. I have seen it happen to more of my peers than I care to count.

We are a generation of people who have irreversibly connected the ideas of success and self-esteem with a college education. As this is proving to be false, we are doing nothing to correct this as a culture because it's just too easy to continue promising children the best possible outcome. Perhaps college isn't the best option for everyone, but few people want to say this because it may compromise their child's self-esteem or otherwise make them feel less special than their peers.

Over time, our culture has built towering self-esteem, which has given way to entitlement, which is having a negative impact on the work ethic of younger adults. If a person is certain they are special and have been promised monetary success, it is not difficult to see how he or she could have a diminished work ethic. Entry level positions are of no interest to the majority of my generation. Low level management is the minimum we will accept without some degree of resistance. Because we are obviously and entirely special beings, we no longer have to pay our dues.

Observe young adults in entry-level positions – more often than not they appear to be disgruntled and typically provide a lower level of service than their older counterparts. This is something I have always admired about the Greatest Generation. They tend to have an infallible work ethic. Even now, you still happen upon a member of that generation in the work force every now and again, and no matter what the job is, it's done happily and well. Most of them are working because they find work to be an enjoyable and gratifying experience, which is a feeling that few members of my generation can identify with.

My paternal grandfather was part of the Greatest Generation. He is a man that truly embodied all of the positive qualities of his generation, and I will always be proud that he is my namesake. He began working on his family farm as a child in elementary school. After he graduated from high school, he was drafted for service in World War II, which cost him a basketball scholarship to Wake Forest University and his only opportunity to attend college. He reported for service, completed his training and was honorably discharged shortly thereafter due to the resolution of the war. He returned home and opened a small grocery store and gas station.

For the next five decades, he opened his store every morning before six and closed between seven and eight in the evening. Sundays were his only day off. Somehow, he found time to help his brother run the family farm as well. There was a stove in the back of his store, where he would cook meals for his wife and five children. He made the decision to close the store in 2002 and passed away in 2009. I never heard him voice a single complaint. He was always happy to do his work, and always did it well. Work was not simply a means to an end for him and his kind.

The largest difference between our generations is that the Great Depression fundamentally shaped the Greatest Generation. What success they found in life was rarely given to them. Nobody told them they were special. Nobody cared how they felt about themselves.

People of that time were much more concerned with how to feed their family, or keep a job. Even after the lingering effects of the Depression faded, World War II became an American concern, further preventing parents and adults from worrying about the self-esteem of children.

Conversely, Generation Y and the Millennials were born during a time of unmatched prosperity. Not only were we no longer concerned with obtaining enough food, we were fighting a losing battle against obesity and Type II Diabetes. There was a war going on in the nineties, but it didn't seem to be a huge concern or have much impact on our day to day lives. There was so very little to worry about that we had to make up something to fret over.

That's how the human brain works. We were prey for so long that we have an impulsive need to worry. From an evolutionary standpoint, prey animals that are more alert (read: anxious) are more likely to survive and reproduce. Over time, this creates entire species of animals that are predisposed to be worrisome. It's the emotional equivalent of the appendix, a vestigial souvenir from a time when we still remembered that are just another kind of mammal. But I digress.

Since there was nothing else to worry about, we perseverated about the well-being of our children. What if our children don't feel good about themselves? What if having winners makes the losers feel badly about themselves? What if having less than the highest self-esteem imaginable results in unhappy adults? Everyone gets a trophy. Everyone should feel special at all times.

A few years ago, I found myself in a supervisory position over a number of other therapists and mental health professionals. During my brief and frustrating tenure in this role, I noticed that several employees would simply ignore the aspects of their job that they felt were beneath them. Unfortunately for me, I was held accountable for their shortcomings, but also never allowed to fire any of them no matter how strong my case. One therapist refused to make calls to remind clients of upcoming appointments or to reschedule missed appointments. Because of this, her productivity was abysmal, and she never generated more than half of her own salary, all of which she consistently blamed on her clients' poor attendance. She adopted an external locus of control, and by citing outside factors, she felt no responsibility to rectify this issue.

More than one employee refused to do essential paperwork that allowed the company to bill for the services they provided to our clients, resulting in high productivity that was all but meaningless to the business. Another would not do notes until his charts were about to be audited, which cost the business money through fines on multiple occasions. It probably isn't necessary to point out that this company was not very successful, and ultimately closed because of the owner's inability to effectively address the entitlement in her employees. This represents my fear if this level of entitlement persists – offices and factories will be populated with people giving their work very little effort because they feel better than they actually are.

Another instance of this is a friend of mine who graduated from high school early to enroll in the UTI NASCAR Tech program. His ambition was to work in the home garage of a NASCAR team. He ultimately wanted to be one of the engine builders, but was actually not picky about what he did as long as he worked in the garage. He did very well in the program, and even took the initiative to work at a coffee shop frequented by many drivers and crew chiefs, where he successfully networked and established relationships with them.

After graduation he received two job offers without interviewing, both of which represented an entry-level position in NASCAR – he would travel with the pit crew to the races. He expressed his interest in working in the home garage over pit crew and told that he had to pay his dues for a few years and work his way up to the garage. He chose to decline both offers, probably in part because he believed (consciously or unconsciously) that his ability was above working his way up to the position he wanted.

For years, society had told him that he was special and gifted and better than others, just like it had told the rest of us. Suddenly adulthood pulled back the curtain and he was unable to integrate the conflicting truths presented to him. He never found work in the automotive industry.

People of younger generations have been force fed self-esteem to the point that they will only give a cursory effort to anything perceived as beneath them. They deserve a promotion based on their inherent and obvious worth, not due to their ability to demonstrate proficiency and talent beyond their current position. They are entitled to a high paying position because they are entitled to it. And the Ouroboros continues to devour its tail.

FICTIONAL IMPLICATIONS

Eric Cartman will have you know that he is most certainly not fat, he just happens to have bigger bones than most other people. The sociopathic terror of South Park Elementary School is a caricature of the Self-Esteem Movement. He is lazy, aggressive, entitled, and feels that he is objectively better than others. Murderous tendencies aside, he could easily be any number of children in schools across America. Eric Cartman represents one of the worst-case scenarios when discussing the implications of the Self-Esteem Movement.

Cartman's inflated sense of self-esteem is largely his mother's doing. She appears to feel guilty about his absent father, so adopted an incredibly indulgent parenting style, presumably to 'make up' for this. She tells him he is special. She assures him that he is big boned instead of overweight. She consistently excuses his behavior to everyone, most importantly to herself. Cartman behaves in any way he chooses because his mother is terrified to correct him, since this might invalidate his feelings of specialness and invite the sort of rage that can only come from questioning the uniqueness of a snowflake. As a result, he has become nothing short of diabolical.

Ms. Cartman's indulgence knows no bounds. To prevent Cartman from becoming angry and feeling like he is not the most special entity in the room, she buys him birthday gifts to open at other children's birthday parties. She ensures that he has anything he wants, which is seemingly every new electronic gadget, all while having the second lowest income at the school, only above that of the McCormick family. It is commendable that she puts the needs of her child before her own needs, but immediately giving her son anything he desires has very little to do with his needs. Giving a child everything they want as soon as they want it is a key ingredient in the recipe for horrible and demanding children like Eric Cartman.

The question that too often goes unasked is what makes a child like Eric Cartman special? Nothing. Nothing at all. He is an exaggeration of all of the creatures of the Self-Esteem Movement – shallow, entitled, arrogant, impulsive, and indulgent beings. In order to maintain the illusion of specialness, or at the very least to feel special by comparison, he frequently has to attempt to make others feel less special. He constantly berates Kenny for being poor, Kyle for being Jewish, and Butters for being Butters. Cartman responds violently when his feelings of specialness are challenged in any way, a trait that is becoming increasingly apparent in our own, completely unanimated society.

Cartman is often verbally aggressive and spiteful toward anyone who deals a blow to his self-esteem. When he is publically embarrasses by Scott Tenorman,

Cartman requires vengeance. With the detached and methodical precision of a serial killer, Cartman kills Tenorman's parents, cooks them into a delicious chili, and serves it to him publicly. Obviously, Eric Cartman's feelings of specialness are not to be questioned. Despite his outward bravado and confidence, he is shown on a number of occasions to be quite fragile and in need of the validation of others to maintain his feelings of self-worth. This is common in people who possess the sort of confidence that is manufactured instead of earned.

Society has led Ms. Cartman to believe that her son deserves feelings of specialness, and she must do any and everything in her power to ensure that he feels special, and has the highest self-esteem her money can buy. She knows that she has completely lost control of her son, but is helpless to change it at this point. Eric is not special, but he knows that he is, and will not be told otherwise. If this level of negative impact is observable in truly unspecial beings, what happens if the child actually *is* special in some way?

Kenny Powers is (arguably) not a child, however, all of the qualities that define Kenny Powers have been groomed and refined since childhood. HBO's *Eastbound and Down* follows the aftermath of the disaster that was Kenny Powers' Major League Baseball pitching career. The more asinine qualities of his personality were certainly exacerbated by his fame, but the truth is he was probably always an unrelenting asshole. One must assume that Kenny Powers always excelled at baseball. He was most likely told he was special by his parents, coaches, peers, and many of the small town adults that love athletic children.

Kenny Powers always knew he was special and behaved as such. He became cocky and arrogant because he believed himself to be better than everyone around him. High school was most likely an easy endeavor for Powers, where coaches leveraged teachers and administrators to keep him out of trouble and keep his GPA over a certain mark to ensure he was able to continue playing ball. No matter how oblivious Kenny Powers was (and is) to the feelings of those around him, he knew that he was treated differently than his peers because of his talent for throwing balls at high velocity. He received special treatment because of his talents, which meant that he actually was special. His habit of lording over friends and acquaintances like a white trash monarch probably began during high school.

Eastbound and Down begins years after Kenny Powers learned of his specialness. At its core, the show chronicles the extreme difficulty Powers has coping with the fact that he is no longer special, and realizing that he is probably objectively worse than most people. The series begins with a montage of his career in the majors, consisting of displays of his arrogance and quickly throwing his arm out. Because he knew with conviction that he was the best thing to ever happen to baseball, he was blind to the fact that his career would not be a long one. When confronted with evidence of his waning abilities, Powers would either blame someone or something else for his poor performance, or become aggressive.

Once he is forced to move home in a state of semi-disgrace, Kenny Powers continued to behave like the big shot major league pitcher he used to be. He is unable to successfully integrate the *actual truth* with *his truth*. In his mind he is still a famous professional athlete, even though he is (at various times) a drug addled PE teacher, a Mexican minor league baseball player, or a salesman at a car rental agency.

Kenny Powers was conditioned to believe that he could behave in any way he wanted to, that he was entitled to fame, would always receive preferential treatment, and was better than everyone else. Because of this, he becomes angry when people do not continue to condone this behavior well after he stopped being special. Kenny Powers used to be special, and damn it he will continue to be special regardless of facts.

One of the stranger truths about Kenneth Powers is that he is probably less obnoxious during the course of the series than he was as a professional baseball player. His behaviors became slightly less arrogant because they were not being reinforced. However, the general perception is that he is infinitely less bearable after his career had ended. The only real explanation for this is that we excuse all varieties of undesirable behavior in those who are special by way of being famous. While Kenny was famous, his self-righteous arrogance was considered acceptable, and even encouraged.

Children are capable of noticing that special or famous people are held to a different standard, which is often much more lenient with regard to social constructs and rules. These children are also being ceaselessly told that they are special. It is only logical that some of them associate these two norms and begin acting as though they are better than others, and rules have no bearing on their own actions, rewards, or consequences.

Joffrey Baratheon, first of his name, King of Westeros. One of the most universally despised characters in *Game of Thrones,* no small achievement in a series that is rife with despicable personalities. From his introduction, he is exponentially more arrogant and horrible. Unfortunately for everyone living in Westeros at the time, Joffrey *was* actually special. He was a prince and became king at a young age. By definition, kings are special. However, being born into the correct family at the correct time is (usually) the only thing special about the people who become kings.

Presumably from birth, Joffrey's mother took every opportunity to remind him of precisely how special he was. After all, he was the product of joining two wealthy and powerful families, and would be king. He would have nearly limitless power, and must be obeyed at all times. As a child, his mother would not allow his behavior to be corrected by anyone, including his father. Years before taking the throne, Joffrey was already making demands as though he were king. When these demands were not met with unwavering immediacy, Joffrey would sulk, brood, or tantrum until his impulses were satisfied.

King Robert, the man Joffrey believed to be his father, taught his son that kings were men of action.

Kings took what they wanted and allowed none to stand in their way. Disrespect would not be tolerated. Kings did anything they wanted, and usually in excess. King Robert's fondness of wine and whores were not things that he attempted to hide. He was a king, and did exactly as he pleased. Joffrey learned from his parents that he was entitled to supreme power, instantaneous satisfaction of his impulses, and justified to act in any way he saw fit. If someone was bold enough to challenge his authority, he need only speak and that person would find themselves lacking a tongue, or perhaps a head.

Even after taking the crown, Joffrey remained a petulant and vicious boy. He typically refuses the advice of his council and is unnecessarily cruel, especially to Sansa Stark, who he is supposed to wed. This becomes abundantly clear when he promises mercy for her father, only to have him beheaded in her presence, and forcing her to visit his rotting head atop the castle gates.

Joffrey has Sansa beaten frequently for answering questions inappropriately and for the 'treasons' of her family. After she is no longer required to marry him, he informs her that he intends to rape her at his leisure, and no one will stop him. He also has an inexplicably strong desire to serve her the head of her brother at his wedding feast. An impulse that was only quelled by his grandfather, the only man in the realm capable of sending the king to bed without his supper.

While Sansa Stark serves as the most consistent and obvious example of Joffrey's unyielding cruelty, there are dozens of examples that could be pointed out.

He demands a knight be drowned in wine for arriving at a tournament drunk. After receiving a crossbow as a gift, he fires it into a crowd of people begging for bread at the castle gates. He calls his personal knight 'dog' and orders him around as such. He publicly ridicules his uncle on numerous occasions, usually for being a dwarf. A scene appearing only in the television series shows Joffrey receiving two whores as a gift from his uncle, only to force one to beat the other for his amusement.

Despite his penchant for violence and cruelty, it is worth noting that Joffrey rarely does anything at all. He orders for death and violence to be carried out in his name. The king tantrums when his work is not done in a satisfactory manner, but usually cannot be bothered to hold court or attend his own council meetings. Joffrey feels entitled to all the benefits of being king with none of the work or responsibility. His subjects must show unyielding loyalty, but he should not have to earn this with gallantry or any sort of benevolent action. His enemies should suffer, but this should require nothing that would be potentially tiring.

If things are not exactly as Joffrey thinks they should be, if he feels less than an all-powerful ruler, he responds with childish rage. This is consistent with a person who has been taught that reward comes without work, a person who feels that they deserve more than others. Respect and admiration are given, not earned. In Joffrey's case, he is instilled with these values by both his heritage and his mother's reckless indulgence. A king is special. A king who thinks himself special does not a good king make. His untimely end is neither unexpected nor sad. It is not surprising that no one aside from his mother grieves for him.

Game of Thrones author, George R. R. Martin, describes Joffrey as an amalgamation of some of the children he attended school with. He says that Joffrey is like them in that he is a "classic bully" all of whom were "incredibly spoiled." Like Eric Cartman, Joffrey is an exaggerated account of the real world implications of the Self-Esteem Movement. Think about the children sitting in middle school classrooms right now. They have been told they are special, that they deserve anything they can dream of, they should not have to wait for what they want, and they will always win. Now take a moment to consider what would happen if one of those children were given control of a continent.

Anakin Skywalker was the product of immaculate conception. There has never been an example of this in which the child was not incredibly special; they are often gods or demigods of some kind. It is essentially mythological shorthand ensuring that everyone is aware that the child will be important in some way or another.

Anakin was a gifted and intelligent child who had the ability to sense things before they happened. Upon meeting him, Jedi Master Qui-Gon Jinn found that Anakin had an extremely high number of midi-chlorians. For the less dorky among us, midi-chlorians are what give Jedi the ability to tap into The Force and do all their cool Jedi stuff. It is assumed at this point that Anakin is the prophesized chosen one who will forever bring balance to The Force. Much the same as immaculate conception, anybody who is the subject of a prophecy is probably objectively special.

Essentially everyone is aware of the story from here. As he ages, Anakin becomes an incredibly powerful Jedi Knight. He is seduced by the dark side, the chosen envoy of which is a creepy old senator for some reason. His anger is exploited. His power becomes arrogance. And he ultimately becomes Darth Vader, but only after being chopped to bits by Obi Wan Kenobi on the side of a volcano. The high ground, it seems, is the key to winning a lightsaber duel. That is the story as it is told to us, but the underlying factors that potentially contributed to his Luciferian fall from grace are much more interesting.

Anakin Skywalker began his life as a slave, but was aware that he was special even then. He knows of his miraculous birth, and is aware that other people cannot see into the future. His mother reinforces these feelings of specialness, as mothers are wont to do, especially when there is something actually making their child special.

Enter the Jedi. Suddenly, Anakin is so special that there may be a prophecy about him. He has the potential to be one of the most powerful beings in the galaxy, and may be special enough to save everyone and everything in said galaxy. This is a lot of information for a nine-year-old to process.

As Anakin grows and becomes more powerful, his confidence also grows. He has certainly internalized the idea that his power and success have been prophesized, and are therefore an unquestionable guarantee. Slowly, he begins to feel that the rulings of the Jedi Council should have no bearing on his actions. He feels justified in anything he does, including murdering an entire village of sand people. He is special, and is aware of exactly how special he is. He is entitled to respect and demands it from anyone he meets, including the Jedi Masters responsible for his training. Anakin will not be denied anything, and refuses to compromise. It does not take long for his confidence to fester into arrogance. He begins to act impulsively while holding himself in higher regard than anyone else.

The reason that it was easy for young Anakin to succumb to the dark side can be boiled down to one very simple reason: the Jedi stopped validating his feelings of specialness. He spent the entirety of his childhood hearing about how special he was. How he was the chosen one. How he might one day save the galaxy. Once it became clear that this was most likely not the case, the Jedi significantly reduced how much they reinforced his (extremely inflated) self-esteem. His future became clouded once he stopped feeling so special. They began to reprimand his actions and caution him against acting out of anger or arrogance. Predictably, this only served to make him make him angrier and more arrogant than he already was.

Agents of the dark side seized this opportunity to sway Anakin. Palpatine befriends him, and begins to exploit the young Jedi's need for validation. He assures Anakin that he is special and that the rules should not apply to him as they do to others. He reminds Anakin of how powerful he can become and suggests that the Jedi Council is certainly fearful of his potential. Over time, he convinces Anakin that the council is plotting against him and planning to take over the republic, which served as his primary motivation for turning to the dark side in the original draft of the prequel films.

Anakin believed himself to be better than his peers (and his masters), and Palpatine took advantage of every opportunity to reinforce this idea. Because the dark side was validating Anakin's truths and the Jedi were challenging them, he chose to spare Palpatine and kill Samuel L. Jackson instead, which is a completely unforgiveable decision.

Anakin Skywalker was an extremely special person, even if he was not the subject of a prophecy. His downfall was hubris and nothing more. Qui-Gon hoped that Anakin would bring balance to the force. Ironically, the communication Anakin received from his masters as a child was anything but balanced.

I suppose one could say the same about George Lucas. He was met with much praise in his early career, all of which he deserved. Until the release of *Episode I* in 1999, he was held in the highest regard by nerds across the world. For two decades, he was told without question that he was special because he had made this wonderful thing for the world to enjoy. The problem began once he started making the prequels, which I never completely understood, since I don't think the prequels are actually *that* bad. Sure, they are muddled and clumsy in places, but they could have easily been good movies.

By the time that Lucas made the prequels he had already internalized the idea that he was incapable of failure. Success was a guarantee. He knew this because for twenty years the entire world had showered him with praise. Nobody stood up to Lucas during the making of the films, or if they did, he was apparently not receptive to it. Like Anakin, George began his career being extremely special, which was the ultimate cause of his undoing.

Luke Skywalker bears mentioning as more than just Anakin's son. Luke is factually more important than his father, because the prophecy actually was about him. Despite gaining this knowledge, Luke never behaves arrogantly. This is in part because Obi-Wan and Yoda had years to learn from their mistakes with Anakin prior to their interactions with Luke. He is told he is special, but not better than others. They are much more realistic with him than they had been with his father. By exercising moderation in their training and communication with Luke, he becomes a more self-aware and authentic person who is not as easily swayed to the dark side as his father had been.

Eric Cartman is not special in any way. Kenny Powers used to be special, but isn't special anymore. Joffrey Baratheon is special, but only by birth. Anakin Skywalker was an incredibly special child, and Luke Skywalker is the most special of them all. Ironically, Luke is also the only decent person among them.

Being special is nearly irrelevant. How you perceive yourself in relation to others is of much greater importance. If a person knows with conviction that they are so unbelievably special that it makes them better than others, then that person is probably an insufferable douchebag who might try to take over the galaxy, kill all the gingers, and/or ruin everything for the rest of us in some way or another.

Life imitates art, but art also imitates life. Both statements are painfully applicable in this argument. As the Self-Esteem Movement gained ground, the portrayal of humanity on television and in film has changed. With the exception of Luke Skywalker, each character discussed was conceptualized and given life after we had succumbed to self-esteem. They are all (potentially) unintentional caricatures of our society, and there is an unfortunate amount of truth in any caricature. Impulsive, arrogant, and entitled people watching impulsive, arrogant, and entitled characters will only perpetuate the existence of both.

FEAR AND LOATHING ON THE INTERNET

The internet has played a vital role in perpetuating the negative values of the Self-Esteem Movement. The point in time where everyone started being special coincides with the advent of the internet as we know it. It is important that these things happened in tandem, because the children being told they were special were also the first people to really use the internet beyond forwarding chain emails.

Suddenly in the nineties, there was this new and uncharted thing that could be used as a platform to spew our every compulsion into the eternally expanding void of our collective unconscious. Even in the dark ages of dial up, adolescents saw that the internet infinitely extended their reach, and their ability to share their specialness with others. Validation of specialness was easily quantified. The number of emails you get in a day. The number of friends on your IM contact lists. The number of hits to your geocities website.

Currently the biggest perpetrators are Facebook and YouTube. Facebook is a cultural force unlike anything I have ever seen. I have a Facebook account. Of course I have one. I remember when it arrived at my college and the startling pace with which it became a vital part of socialization on campus. Presently, I log onto my account a few times per week to return any messages I've received and browse the news feed, which I still consider new and obnoxious. What Facebook has become is a place for people to force themselves and their thoughts into my life while I'm sitting on the toilet.

What you cooked for dinner, your list of errands, why the cashier upset you on those errands, your political or social views, the current weather, inadvertent TV or movie spoilers, your opinion on whatever sporting event is or has just happened, anything that could be called 'drama,' and just about everything else put into Facebook status updates are irrelevant and useless information to everyone but the person typing them. We somehow feel important enough that we chronicle every mundane detail of our existence for several hundred of our closest friends, acquaintances, coworkers, and strangers we may have met at a party once.

Self-esteem is again quantified in a numerical format – how many friends do I have? How many likes will this status get? How many comments? People will then reflexively check their Facebook account to track this numeric representation of their specialness.

I have seen pictures of newborn babies, posted by the mother less than an hour after delivery. If that fails to lend credibility to the idea that we are all impulsively seeking out external validation, I don't know what does. We crave validation so badly that many of us document our life in favor of living it.

I don't understand Twitter at all. I am aware of

71

what it is and how it works, but I just cannot grasp why people use it. I have never even seen the website, aside from screen captures when some celebrity manages to embarrass themselves in less than 140 characters, and it warrants news coverage. At its core, Twitter is a place where we are given an audience for our every thought and musing. It doesn't pretend to do anything outside of catering to our incessant need for attention, the honesty of which is admirable. It's driven by nothing more than the promise of validation and a skewed concept of fame. Unfortunately, the fact that some (maybe most) people aren't deserving of an audience has been lost beneath the cultural avalanche of the Self-Esteem Movement.

Facebook, Twitter, and internet culture in general are partially responsible for the migration of many of the norms and values of the Self-Esteem Movement into other generations. Once Facebook left the confinement of college campuses and everyone you've ever met registered, it became clear that the specialness and entitlement of the younger generations were seeping into the older generations. This may be due to older people emulating the behaviors and norms that were pre-established on the site, and gradually internalizing them. The other possibility is a function of resentment toward the younger generations – like when an older child regresses upon the arrival of a new baby. *Look at me, I'm special too.*

The same can be said of the younger generations. Once every teen and tween created a Facebook account, the norm of posting every fleeting thought as a status update was already in existence. Younger people have always, and will always, emulate people slightly older than themselves. This represents modeling and scaffolding, which are developmentally appropriate behaviors for children and adolescents. By attempting to socialize like people who are slightly more advanced, you become more socially adept. This is the reason the youngest of several children often hits developmental milestones more quickly than their older siblings did – they are constantly working to catch up, and then keep up.

Because Facebook was a place where comments, likes, number of friends, and status updates validated feelings of specialness in college students, younger adolescents immediately began to emulate this behavior. They internalized it to a seemingly higher degree than other generations simply because of their age, and their current developmental tasks, which is to learn how to appropriately socialize with others in an adult fashion. We learn to create and maintain relationships, and to balance those relationships with the other areas of life.

Adolescents spending significant portions of their time on social media seeking out quantified self-worth has resulted in age appropriate social skills being neglected and left to rot on the vine. These are the people who cannot appropriately manage anything more than small talk unless they can communicate via text or Facebook message. If this pattern continues on its current trajectory, there will be fewer and fewer people modeling appropriate communication and self-disclosure skills for younger generations.

Another aspect of the Facebook that has an effect on self-esteem and the Self-Esteem Movement is the ability for each of us to control how we are perceived by others. We are now our own personal brands; and like any responsible business owner, we gear our actions toward protecting, promoting, and growing that brand. Everyone has an actual self and an ideal self, which represents the self that we aspire to be. Facebook (and any other sort of social media) allows its users to present an idealized version of their self and their life. This is natural human behavior to a degree, proven by the fact that we generally answer positively when asked how we are doing on any given day. So, it's not necessarily harmful that people are making their lives seem better than they actually are. How it is perceived, and by whom, is where the problem lies.

When life happens to be less than glamorous, the denizens of the Self-Esteem Movement brood and lament about the average, semi-successful life they have been able to achieve. These people spend a significant amount of time on Facebook (as most people presently do) and are presented with everyone they have ever met projecting the most idealistic portrait of their life onto the internet. Instead of being rational and accepting that nobody has a perfect life, they default to their core values which have assured them boundless happiness, affluence, and fulfillment.

They believe they are entitled to these things, so much that they believe that these idyllic projections are an accurate representation of the lives of others. They then assume that *they* should be as happy as their friends' carefully coordinated travel pictures, status updates, and check-ins would have you believe that they are. Not surprisingly, these people experience a decrease in feelings of self-worth because the core values of the Self-Esteem Movement discourage rational expectations.

YouTube is a beast of another nature entirely. Soon after it went live, everyone with a camera and an internet connection could, and seemingly did, seek out fame and notoriety. Our culture consistently reminds children that they are special and unique. Of course they believe that fame and fortune is just a few grainy YouTube videos away.

Approximately 60 hours of video per minute were uploaded to YouTube in mid-2012. According to YouTube, that number increased to approximately 100 hours per minute by mid-2013. Some simple but illustrative math makes this already giant number seem even more ridiculous: 6,000 hours per hour, 144,000 hours per day, and more than 1,000,000 hours per week are uploaded to YouTube. That's more than three billion minutes of videos per year. It almost seems impossible that this much content is being uploaded. The site reportedly has more than four billion views each day. Approximately six billion hours of video are viewed each month; meaning that, on average, every person on the planet watches just under an hour of YouTube content each month.

YouTube gives people an audience for whatever it is they want to do. There are videos of people opening new products – only opening them, and offering little in the way of information or review. Just thousands of people wanting to show the internet what they bought. Searching for 'unboxing' brings in just shy of 18 million videos. Millions of people thought their experience was interesting enough to put on the internet for the enjoyment of others. My faith in humanity is dwindling.

There are 147,000 reaction videos for '2 girls 1 cup,' all of which consist of people (including Joe Rogan) looking horrified when shown a video I am thankful to have avoided thus far. Users have posted 44 million video blogs (which is probably a vast underestimation since this number comes from only searching for 'vlog'), 30 million cat videos, 40 million challenge videos, and 28.7 million parody videos. 87.8 million people have made cover songs they felt were good enough to put on the internet, of which 80 million are probably terrible. Searching 'review' yields 95.7 million results. It seems that everyone truly is a critic.

The music video 'Chocolate Rain' has been viewed 93 million times. There is no logical explanation for this. The infamous 'leave Brittany alone' video has been viewed 46.7 million times. Even worse, there are 181,000 results when searching 'leave Brittany alone' many of which are parody videos, which can admittedly be funny when done well. However, nothing has ever been funny 181,000 different times. Most likely there was no new way to parody that video after the fourth or fifth video was uploaded, yet people continued to make them by the hundreds, because they believed that their take on the video was funnier, special, unique, and/or otherwise something that should be seen by the world.

People go as far as documenting their own drug use on YouTube, which is one of the most thoroughly terrible ideas imaginable. Searching for 'salvia' bestows the watcher with 229,000 results, most of which involve people smoking the substance and going briefly insane. The video 'horrible salvia trip' has 3.75 million views. The description reads 'hit me up on Facebook if you like this video,' which is somehow worse than the video itself. He is quite obviously seeking out notoriety and validation through any means necessary.

There is a video of an obese young man, who goes by the name Big Mastadon (his spelling), attempting to eat 40 pizza rolls in under two minutes. It was his first upload, and I am still entirely unclear about why that video was made and intentionally placed on the internet. Despite my confusion, this video has been viewed more than one million times. He has uploaded twenty-one videos at present, with only a few being food challenges of this nature. More recently, it appears that he has been uploading vlogs to talk about his desire to lose weight and progress toward his goal. He has also uploaded a video audition for weight loss show *The Biggest Loser*. Mastadon is using YouTube to seek out public notoriety through a personal goal.

Taking a minute to browse the comments left by others on Big Mastadon's videos reveals another harsh truth about our post-internet society. We are incredibly mean to strangers on the internet, almost all the time.

In the wake of the Self-Esteem Movement, we require frequent and consistent feelings of specialness. To most efficiently achieve this, many people have started trying to reduce positive feelings in other people, but only when those people are total strangers unfortunate enough to stumble into their path online. By reducing the self-worth of others, we increase our own feelings of worth by comparison, which is infinitely easier than working to *actually* increase our own feelings of self-esteem.

Many of the comments left on the Big Mastadon's videos are brutal attacks on him as a person. On one of his most recent videos, in which he talks about losing weight and cheerfully encourages others to do the same, one comment reads, "I hope you die you fat piece of shit." The same can be said for most other videos on the site – hateful, ignorant, xenophobic, and/or racist comments make up quite nearly all comments left on videos. YouTube provides the option to disable comments on your uploaded content, yet he does not take advantage of this feature on any of his videos, despite the negativity and attacks left for him. It seems that he, like so many other people using the site, crave validation so desperately that they will allow anyone with an internet connection to berate them at their leisure.

In addition to the vlogs, reviews, challenges, reactions, and cats, there are thousands upon thousands of videos of people playing an instrument with varying degrees of success. There are just as many horrible homemade hip hop videos for horrible homemade hip hop songs. Just like Facebook, validation is quantified in number of hits and comments. YouTube takes it one degree farther by including a dislike option and a rating scale, allowing you to calculate the exact percentage of your specialness.

The only reasonable explanation for any of the millions of pointless videos on YouTube is that our culture has held self-esteem in such high regard that we all obviously deserve to be famous. We all obviously have something new and exciting and special to offer. We are absolutely entitled to the fifteen minutes of fame that Andy Warhol mumbled about that one time.

Daniel Tosh has built a successful career using only a team of writers, a few laptops, and the wealth of stupidity at his disposal on YouTube. Week after week, he finds dozens of videos to viciously rip apart. Despite this being the show's primary focus, the more interesting and relevant aspect is the weekly guest segment. Occasionally these are profiles of internet sensations like Sweet Brown, Antoine Dodson, or the Chocolate Rain guy. More often, they are web redemptions, where guests who have a popular and embarrassing video come on the show and get to reenact the video in a more successful way. The common theme is that Tosh makes jokes about the video and person for the majority of the segment.

It's generally a true statement that people do not like being made fun of or having jokes made at their expense. Many of the guests on Tosh.0 (especially the web redemption guests) have incredibly embarrassing videos that will draw significantly more attention as a direct result of their participation in the show. If we (safely) assume that the participants are aware of the show and its premise, then we can also assume that the motivation to appear on television outweighs the motivation to avoid further embarrassment.

One of the most plausible explanations for this is that we believe that we are entitled to fame so much so that we will willingly volunteer to be interviewed (read: ridiculed) by a person who is so good at ridiculing things that it's his actual career. Validation at any cost. Sure, I may have broken my legs jumping off of a cliff, or shot myself in the leg making a trick shot video, or wrecked my dad's brand new car into our house, or any number of other real scenarios that were on the show, but at least I'm on television, which makes me more specialer than everyone else who *isn't* on television.

The internet in general has heavily contributed to the entitlement that has become prevalent in our culture. Instant gratification is what the internet is all about. If you want to know the length of the Great Wall of China (13,171 miles), how tall the Empire State Building is (1454 feet), or maybe you have a burning desire to know what year Ozzy Ozbourne was born (1948), you can find out in about six seconds.

Obtaining information or learning historically involved asking someone who might have this information, digging through an encyclopedia, or actually going to a library and doing some research. Now we just need to have the ability to access the internet, which is usually only as difficult as reaching into our pockets or bags. We literally have the ability to learn about anything without getting out of our seat.

Everything in existence can be found online with ease. This unprecedented access to the knowledge of the world has destroyed our cultural sense of wonder. Learning about a new subject no longer has the same pride, since anyone can learn the same things in minutes. We no longer feel good about learning because it takes no effort to do so.

Trial and error is all but dead. Kids (and adults) no longer make attempts and learn from failure, they just pop on YouTube and watch an instructional video. I have had kids proudly tell me that they are great at making paper airplanes (or some other arbitrary example). Being the polite thing to do, I engage them in conversation and ask how they learned to make them. Every single one of them has told me that they learned how to make the best paper airplanes by watching YouTube. They didn't spend a whole day with one of their friends folding hundreds of pieces of paper, slowly improving until their paper airplanes were the envy of their whole neighborhood. Nope. They just all watch the same video and fold the same airplane and feel the same level of nothingness about it.

We are no more than a few seconds away from knowing almost anything we could possibly want to know. Miraculously, nobody is more intelligent because of this. At best we have a trivial or passing knowledge of a wide variety of topics, which serves less as real knowledge and more as a means to sound much, much smarter than you actually are.

Wikipedia is the king of informational instant gratification. Spend five minutes on Wikipedia and you can obtain conversational knowledge of most subjects, provided of course, that the person you are conversing with is operating within the same limited knowledge base. I have taken to calling this Wikismart, and suggest you all do the same.

There are an alarming number of people who will spend a few minutes browsing Wikipedia and purport expert level knowledge based on the factoids they have gleaned from skimming (not even reading) the Wiki article on the subject. This is feeds our culture's level of entitlement and need for instant gratification. Why bother actually gaining real knowledge on a subject when you can *appear* to have expert level knowledge in a fraction of the time. After all, looking intelligent and being intelligent are ostensibly the same thing.

The level of access to information afforded to us by the internet is still amazing to me. However, this borderline magical level of convenient access to anything and everything does not come without a price. People born into our post-internet world have become extremely accustomed to instantaneous satisfaction of their every query. Because of this, they have become impatient in all other areas of their life. We will not wait in line at the bank. We do not want to call customer service and talk to an operator. No, we will not hold please. Mailing a letter and waiting for a response is preposterous. Even email is too slow in some cases. We want it, and we want it right now.

Combine this impulsivity with the sense of entitlement that accompanies the weapons grade confidence that has been refined in children by the Self-Esteem Movement. This generates a startling number of young people who have several core values that are dangerous in combination: I am special and unique, I have inherent worth that is objectively more than that of others, I am entitled to more than others, and I should not have to wait for the things I want.

The co-occurrence of the Self-Esteem Movement and the wide spread adoption of the internet has increased all of the negative qualities that already existed in adolescents of time. Because of this, we have become a culture that thinks too highly of themselves, is largely impatient, and feels entitled to more than their peers based upon their own feelings of self-worth.

REALITY PORNOGRAPHY

Television is arguably the best it has ever been. In the past decade, there have been numerous series that have changed our perception of how good television can be. *Breaking Bad, Mad Men, The Walking Dead, True Detective, House of Cards,* and *Game of Thrones* to name a few. Sitcoms have become more intelligent and the laugh track is all but dead. *Louie* is probably one of the best shows currently on television.

In this new age of television, characters develop and stories arc. Television literally has something (and something good) for everyone at this point. Despite this, I often find myself yearning for days long past. Days in which television was mediocre at best and you had to schedule yourself around your shows; but at least there weren't entire networks devoted to reality television.

Long ago, *The Real World* was an interesting and unique show on MTV. Now it has become increasingly difficult to find a show that is not a reality show. At present, there are no less than four shows dedicated to pawnshops, at least three shows about buying storage units and/or shipping containers, and numerous shows about rich, bitchy housewives living in rich, bitchy cities. There are shows about loggers, fishermen, alligator

hunters, and family duck call businesses. Towing companies have even become a subject of interest. There are
entirely too many shows about teenage pregnancy.

Bridalplasty bears mentioning in isolation since
it might actually be the worst thing ever put on the air,
which is an astounding achievement when one considers
the wealth of garbage presently available on television.
The premise of the show is relatively simple, about a
dozen engaged women are put into a mansion, where
they compete for weekly prizes consisting of small cosmetic surgeries, ultimately hoping to win the grand
prize of a total body overhaul that involves any cosmetic
surgeries their (probably silicon) heart desires. They
also win a 'dream wedding' but let's be honest about this,
that was never the real draw for the contestants.

Bridalplasty embodies the most abysmally callow
aspects of our society. The contestants want to look a
particular way, but have no interest in working towards
that goal. They all want to be pretty and special, and
having an absolutely stupid amount of plastic surgery is
the quickest and easiest way to go about that. Fuck
exercising and developing a personality. The fact that
this show made it to air is undoubtedly a precursor to
the apocalypse.

And then there's *The Jersey Shore*.

I unapologetically love *The Jersey Shore*. My wife
and I watched the entire series. It was our guilty pleasure, and since the show concluded, we have yet to find a
suitable replacement. We probably never will. I continue
to be enamored by the absolute ridiculousness of it all.

The entire series was like staring into a solar eclipse – I know it's bad for me and I know that I will probably go blind, but I felt compelled to watch it.

The thing I have always found fascinating about the cast of *The Jersey Shore*, is that they were all generally unremarkable people prior to the start of the show. They were just people in their twenties and thirties that (mostly) lived with their parents and liked to party. Nothing about that seems deserving of fame, because nothing about that *is* deserving of fame. They were selected and thrown into a shore house together and became famous for being a perfect and glorious Italian-American spectacle. Because of *Jersey Shore* everyone knows what a Guido is, and you are hard pressed to find a person who doesn't know who Snookie or Pauly D. are.

My Nana even watched *Jersey Shore*, but would ferociously deny that fact, which is ridiculous when factoring in her outward and shameless love of daytime courtroom shows. This essentially proves three things: the cultural reach of *The Jersey Shore* (and reality TV in general) is incredibly broad, everyone loves to watch Italians being Italians (also see: *The Real Housewives of New Jersey*), and most importantly; the majority of reality TV is so terrible that even an 80-year-old woman is embarrassed to admit she likes it.

The popularity of reality television baffles most people, even those who find themselves transfixed by it. One of the only plausible explanations for the sheer volume of reality shows piped into homes is that it is incredibly cost effective for networks. Find a group of people or some other entity, seduce them with fame, put it on television, profit. Networks can do this time and time again until they find that one breakout show that sucks everyone in like a heroin addiction that rapidly spirals out of control. The History Channel (which should probably have been stripped of its name by now) found it in *Pawn Stars*, which holds the record for most watched telecast in the history of History. Bravo found it with *The Real Housewives* of whatever awful place the first show originated. *Duck Dynasty* draws millions of viewers to A&E each week. It is a low risk/high reward investment for networks.

Reality television fuels our feelings of specialness and our need for constant recognition. Reality television allows us to stare into our televisions and watch people achieve fame who have no real reason to be famous. Most of these reality stars are not actors, musicians, or notable scholars. Even the actors and musicians that find themselves on reality shows are not exactly at the peak of their careers. The most many of them have to offer is being (somewhat) attractive, and sometimes not even that. They are just people more or less going about their daily lives.

The archetype of reality television fame is the Kardashian family. There are several shows devoted to nothing but chronicling the existence of this family. I still have no idea how or why these people are famous. I know that Robert Kardashian was one of O.J. Simpson's defense attorneys, but he died in 2003 and appears to have little bearing on his daughters' fame. His ex-wife,

Kris married Olympic gold medalist Bruce Jenner, but in my limited exposure to the show, he is at best a sad sack husband who appears to dislike the whole idea of being on television. He has probably grown to dislike his wife and stepchildren as well, which seems both reason-able and justified. They are (or at least appear to be) incredibly wealthy, but this does not necessitate fame. Kim Kardashian is slightly exotic looking and attractive. She also has a sex tape, which is my best and only guess at the origin of the Kardashian family fame.

None of us are foolish enough to believe that reality TV is (or ever was) truly real. We know that these shows are edited to increase entertainment value, and sometimes entirely staged. Most of them even list story editors in the credits. Despite this, we continue to watch them as if they were actually real, because we all want to believe the fundamental thing that reality television represents – we can be famous just for being ourselves.

The timing of the reality television explosion is not a coincidence. Around the turn of the century (which is a phrase you should all start using when talking about the early two thousands) the children who were taught that they were all unique little snowflakes had reached adolescence. Suddenly, the majority of people in their late teens and early twenties knew they were special and knew they deserved more than going to college only to get some regular job and achieve some regular life. They were obviously special enough to be famous for *something*, even though they weren't quite sure what that something actually was.

Before my generation came of age, the people on reality shows were borderline sociopaths. Find some clips of early *Real World* seasons – the only people signing up were generally narcissistic and self-absorbed. They were people to be avoided in the real world. Then Generation Y comes along and collectively decided that we were special enough to be on television too. And so we sent in audition tapes by the thousands. If these people are special, then so am I.

The Real World requires cast members to sign a contract that is completely absurd. Most of the items are standard fare alleviating the network of responsibility if you are injured or die during filming. Things escalate quickly from there, however. Several of the more concerning items include the producers' right to discuss and/or exploit any mental illnesses you may have; they assume no responsibility if you contract an STD, but are kind enough to notify you that no one is screened prior to participation; you grant the producers blanket rights to your life story, which they may intentionally misrepresent; and acknowledge that you may be 'humiliated' or 'portrayed in a false light' at their discretion.

The crowning jewel of *The Real World* contract is an item that acknowledges your understanding that interacting with other cast mates carries the risk of 'nonconsensual physical contact.' Basically, MTV is not responsible if you get raped on their show. Despite this, people attend open casting calls by the hundreds across the country. Apparently, for some people, the desire to be famous outweighs any potential exploitation or sexual assault.

Reality television nicely embodies most of the negative aspects of the Self-Esteem Movement and subsequent aftermath. It reinforces the idea that we are all so completely special that our daily life is interesting enough to put on television. Reality shows ice the cake with a very thick layer of instant gratification. Being famous seems easy and quickly obtainable. After all, none of these assholes on television are doing anything extraordinary. There is no incentive to master a craft in an effort to achieve fame, when being yourself requires so much less work. Reality television has helped to perpetuate a culture that believes that they deserve to be famous simply because they deserve to be famous. Again with the circular logic and the Ouroboros.

Sex tapes are a common theme among reality stars and other celebrities. Kim Kardashian and Paris Hilton both have one, and are more famous because of them. Pamela Anderson and Tommy Lee resuscitated their fame with a sex tape that features them having a lot of hepatitis ridden sex in a lot of different places. John Wayne Bobbitt, yes *that* John Wayne Bobbitt has a sex tape. It's actually called *Uncut*, which is probably the most amusing thing I learned during my tenure as a Randall Graves-esque video store clerk.

Screech from Saved by the Bell has a sex tape and nobody knows why. Hulk Hogan has a sex tape, but at least has the decency to be ashamed of it. Brett Michaels has a sex tape, which I'm pretty sure features Pamela Anderson. Tila Tequila made an easy transition from being famous for no reason to having sex on tape. That's too many examples for me to just think of without so much as a cursory Google search. Which leads me to a couple of conclusions – working in a video store was probably a morally detrimental experience for me, and the popularity of sex tapes and pornography are indicative of a shift in our cultural mindset regarding fame.

Predictably at this point, curiosity overcame me and found a list of known celebrity sex tapes. Highlights of this list include former Teen Mom Farrah Abraham, former senator John Edwards, and former reality star Kendra Wilkinson. Fred Durst and Vince Neil both have sex tapes. Tonya Harding made a sex tape at some point after she became a household name for having Nancy Kerrigan attacked. Nadya Suleman, better known as the Octomom made a professionally produced sex tape, which assuredly represents her final attempts to claw her way into fame.

These names support my presupposed hypothesis on celebrity sex tapes – they happen when your career needs a boost, or you are trying desperately to get (or stay) famous. I suppose there are some that were really accidental and had no additional motives behind them, but those appear to be in the minority. People who have obtained a glimmer of fame feel entitled to keep that fame. If that means they have to fuck someone and put it on the internet, then that is precisely what they are going to do.

Reality television and pornography have never seemed that different to me. They are both comprised of people doing something that everyone can do, and tend to feature people who are at least marginally attractive. It boils down to how badly a person wants to be famous, and what they are willing to do to obtain that fame. With enough determination and ability to compromise one's dignity, anyone can be famous for *something.*

Culturally we have told an entire generation of people that they are extremely special and more deserving than their peers. Other factors have reinforced this idea and suggested that fame is easily obtainable. Say some teenager in Georgia has internalized this idea and decided that they should be famous too. After all, they are an attractive guy or girl. The only catch is that they have no special talents or redeeming qualities.

Out comes the camera. YouTube vlogs uploaded by the dozen. Audition tapes made and sent to any reality show currently casting. Headshots procured and sent to every talent agency known to them. Anything to get discovered. Anything for fame. Soon, anything actually starts to mean *anything.*

Suppose that months, or even years go by without achieving fame. Most people would simply give up and acknowledge that fame is not so easily achieved, but there are a few who refuse to give up on their dreams. They may find themselves moving down to Miami and shooting low budget porn, probably with ambitions to make higher budget porn, become famous, and maybe make the transition into film, television, or some other form of sexless entertainment. Well, maybe not sexless, but at least penetration-less.

Somewhere between the inception and realiza-tion of this goal, she may find herself kneeling on an ottoman waiting to be fucked by half a dozen men before they all ejaculate on her, get high, order take out, and go home for the day. Or if this hypothetical person happens to be a guy, then he finds himself standing around, half-heartedly stroking himself, waiting to fuck some girl in tandem with several guys he may have just met.

After Porn Ends is a documentary that profiles several people who have made a career in the adult industry. Typical of most documentaries of this type, it is extremely interesting and slightly sad. The film spends quite a bit of time focusing on the idea that some people are emotionally equipped for being in porn, and some are not. Some people thrive on the power and validation, while others are forever broken by the experience.

Although it is never explicitly stated, many of the stories told in the film imply that the adult industry trades on feelings of specialness and validation. It seems that young people entering porn, especially women are showered with attention, validation, and reminders of their specialness. As time progresses, these validations are withheld or increased to get them to perform acts that they may be resistant to doing.

The most interesting person featured in the doc-umentary is Kimberly Halsey, better known as Houston. She appears to be a likeable and good-natured person. She also holds the world record for 'largest gangbang.' *The Houston 620* is a pornographic film in which she (allegedly) performs sex acts with 620 different people.

Firsthand accounts of the filming estimate the number of people involved to be closer to 100, which is still way, way too many.

Halsey says that she knew that she was going to be a star and decided to have the largest gangbang in history to achieve this. Nobody agrees to something like this, much less generates the idea on their own, unless they are actively seeking fame and validation through any means possible. She also mentions that it was a natural impulse to auction off her leftover bits on her website after her viginoplasty.

Although Halsey's example resides at the far end of the spectrum, the film suggests that actresses in the adult industry regularly do equivalent things. Porn enthusiasts can purchase the panties right off of their favorite starlet during conventions and appearances. I doubt the additional earnings from this significantly improves their standard of living. The only reasonable explanation is that selling their panties to strangers, who will probably have them in their mouth before they reach the parking lot, increases their self-esteem. Most people have never had a stranger ask for the underwear they were currently wearing, and certainly haven't been offered money for them. Because they are in a position where this does happen to them, they may feel more unique and special as a result.

Pornography serves a purpose similar to reality television for the people featured. You are the center of attention. You are on a screen. People are watching you. They are probably a little ashamed of watching it. You are arguably famous to some people. In a very unhealthy way, having sex with strangers, while strangers film it, and more strangers watch it and masturbate validates the fundamental truth that these people have been told most of their lives – I am special and entitled to fame.

I feel compelled to point out that I am in no way suggesting that all children who are told they are special seek out a career in the adult industry. However, it's really not hard to see how the combination of focusing on high self-esteem, holding reality television in such high regard, and the insane amount of readily accessible pornography on the internet can result in a significantly higher number of people that consider porn a viable path on their quest for validation.

Most of us will never be famous for anything. Not only that, but most of us *shouldn't* be famous. Until the onset of the Self-Esteem Movement, the overwhelming majority of us were okay with this reality. Since then, we have become a culture that scrambles toward the limelight with any and every opportunity. Not only will we be famous, we deserve it, and will not be told otherwise.

COUNTERCULTURAL PHYSICS

For every action, there is an equal and opposite reaction. This is true in my limited understanding of physics, and in many instances holds true socially and culturally. The D.A.R.E. program raised awareness about the dangers of drug use. The drug culture seemed to rally in response to this and drug taking increased. 2 Live Crew owe much of their career to the parental advisory sticker. A semi-underground band gains some degree of fame or notoriety, and everyone who knew about them prior to this starts to hate them. Nirvana is still a bad word in the Pacific Northwest.

Countercultures have always existed; some group or another that goes against the grain of society. Wonderfully and obnoxiously, they help mainstream culture to develop and evolve. They prevent our culture from becoming a bland Orwellian society by introducing new fashion, music, art, film, and vernacular. This is in no way an attack on countercultures as a whole as they are necessary and terrible things. However, every large counterculture that has developed since the Self-Esteem Movement began has been more obnoxious than the last.

In the nineties, there were gothic kids. They dressed in black, listened to industrial or eighties pop music, smoked cigarettes, were generally quiet, and wanted to be left alone. For some reason this scared the bejesus out of everyone over the age of thirty, but they were really just being slightly different from everyone else. They were the first opposite and equal reaction to the Self-Esteem Movement. If the snowflakes are fluffy, colorful, and optimistic, then I will be blunt, blackened, and brooding. If everyone is special, then I want to be the anti-special.

Gothic kids intentionally refused to engage in what was expected of them, just to establish themselves as different from the 'preps' or 'jocks' or 'sheep' or whatever group that particular group of gothic kids decided to label and dislike. This was their way to establish themselves as special. In a not so subtle way, gothic kids drank the snowflake Kool-Aid just like everyone else. They were the opposite of special, putting them in the extreme minority, which made them more special and unique by default. It's the same level of elitism that my current favorite counterculture (bearded, vested, underground metal fans) is currently exhibiting as their scene is being slowly encroached by the mainstream.

As the number of gothic kids dwindled, hoards of emo kids quietly shuffled in to fill the cultural gap. For those who have somehow managed to avoid contact with this subset of people, emo is simply short for emotional. Stereotypical emo kids had stupid swoopy haircuts, comically small shirts, and usually wore cuffed and/or skinny jeans. Bright colors, lip rings, white belts, and thick eyeliner all became emo stereotypes as well.

There are entire genres of music that are associated with emo, but to be fair there was a particular style of music that spawned the culture. The original emo music was allegedly born from the hardcore and punk scene in Washington D.C. in the late eighties and early nineties. What emo music became was more in line with bands like Dashboard Confessional, emotionally charged music that was usually overly literal.

Since that time, many other subgenres of music became associated with emo culture, the worst by a wide margin being screamo, which generally has somewhat heavy instrumentation, melodic singing and screaming, unexplained and inexcusable use of autotune in some instances, and breakdowns galore. Screamo became an influence on many other subgenres, which I universally refer to as shitcore instead of learning all of their names.

Emo kids were the first counterculture that I can remember everyone loving to hate, and I'm not entirely sure why. Maybe it was because they were easy to hate, or because the presence of countercultures threaten the norms of the majority. By being different, emo culture threatened the belief that we are all special and unique.

Emo kids seemed to revel in being different than the 'popular kids.' Much like the gothic culture, they established themselves as special by refusing to be like other people. Instead of trying to look despondent or evil, emo kids differentiated themselves by being socially and emotionally different than other people, while still ensuring they looked different enough to stand out in a non-threatening way. I am more aware of my emotions than others are, therefore I am special. Since everyone is special, and I'm identifiably different, I'm even more special than I was before I got this ridiculous haircut.

As emo culture waned, it gave way to the current breed of hipsters. Oh, hipsters; the ever evolving culture that refuses to quit. The unrelenting tenacity of hipster culture is its most, and probably only, admirable quality. Everyone I know at this point either has accused someone of being a hipster, or been accused of being a hipster. Most people find it an incredibly insulting accusation for whatever reason.

Most recently, I was accused of being a hipster for voicing a differing opinion while simultaneously wearing a plaid shirt and having a mustache. Of course, there was nothing sincere about the mustache. There is no such thing as a serious mustache on a person who isn't a father, a villain, or over the age of fifty. But a mustache alone does not a hipster make.

Hipster culture is a hard one to pin down. It is primarily associated with an evolution of indie music culture. No currently accurate stereotypes exist about hipster fashion, which is a statement that is remarkably always true. Williamsburg has become something of a hipster collective. The same can be said for places like Portland and Austin, meaning that the best (and maybe only) way to define the current fashion trends of this culture is to sit in one of these meccas of hipsterdom for a bit and observe the ever evolving definition of hipster.

At any given time hipsters have been associated with plaid shirts, skinny jeans, beards, thick rimmed glasses, Pabst Blue Ribbon, records, cassette tapes, American Apparel, mustaches, fixed gear bicycles, vintage *everything*, irony of any kind, Urban Outfitters, suspenders, year round knit caps, coffee, dressing like a 1930's factory worker, smoking fashionable cigarettes, and veganism. There is no rhyme. There is no reason. But there is a reason for that.

Hipster fashion appears to be so chaotic because it is. Significant value has been placed on being different – and if you can't be different, then you can at least look different. This has seemingly caused the escalating ridiculousness of hipster fashion. Probably right now, there is an individual in one of the aforementioned hipster Meccas wearing a monocle, riding a unicycle, in a camouflage bowler hat that was custom ordered and made from decidedly vintage World War II era fatigues. Combat free, of course. Obviously, this is in an effort to differentiate himself from his friend who often wears Franklin-era bifocals while roller skating and wearing vintage powder blue tuxedo pants. It is a fashion arms race to establish uniqueness at all costs.

Fashion is the common thread that binds many countercultures together. They all have a fashion sense that differs from that of the majority. We like to discuss ways in which countercultures have norms and values that deviate from the majority culture. However, when we think about countercultures, it usually has much more to do with outward appearance than norms. Values define their culture, but a stranger can't necessarily see your values from across the room.

THE SNOWFLAKE EFFECT

Having fashion that is decidedly different than the majority means that anyone who sees you knows that you are different (and better) than them. We have been told that we are special and unique snowflakes to the point that we are all desperately striving to prove that individuality. This means that countercultures adopt pseudo-uniforms to outwardly display their uniqueness simply because looking different is much easier to do than demonstrating how your disparate values actually make you different.

As much as I could go on about hipster fashion, the primary aspect of what makes hipsters culturally relevant to my argument has very little to do with their fashion. The common aspects that seem to unite all hipsters is an almost militant elitism, and (to a lesser extent) vicious snark and/or irony.

We all have a friend that knows about all sorts of underground bands, cult movies, obscure books, and other things that 'you've probably never heard of.' I am that friend to many people due to my fondness of all things stoner/doom/sludge rock/metal, which remains somewhat obscured from the mainstream. Hipsters actively seek out things from the underground for the sake of knowing about them before they 'break.' They love to brag about being at shows with 'only a handful of people' that represented the band when it was 'pure.' Prized possessions usually include the first limited pressing of whatever band is the current being praised in all the most important underground blogs.

In some instances, this strong infatuation with

the underground has very little to do with any actual enjoyment of the material, and much more to do with the feeling of elitism that accompanies knowing about the next darlings of the underground before the rest of the hipsters catch on. By 'liking' as many budding bands on Facebook in whatever underground scene is currently most popular, hipsters can increase their chances of being an early supporter for bands that do 'make it' to any degree. This makes them feel special. It validates their self-observed refined taste in 'authentic' music. It makes them objectively better than everyone else.

Hipsters (and everyone else ferociously obsessed with the underground) validate their feelings of special-ness by establishing themselves as better than their peers with their elitist attitude regarding music (among other things). I must feel special, and if that means pretending to like horrible bands and then talking down to my friends who are unaware of them, then that is precisely what I will do.

Irony and snark are certainly not confined to the hipster culture, although it appears to be a defining characteristic of what makes a hipster a hipster. All hipsters are ironic, but not all ironic people are hipsters, kind of like squares and rectangles. A sense of irony has become synonymous with wearing things in a non-serious way, liking things for reasons outside of their intended purpose, and generally coating your existence in a thick, sticky layer of sarcasm.

My brother in law, Eric has no less than two shirts with depictions of The Macho Man Randy Savage.

He also has a shirt featuring a cat dressed like Eazy-E. My other brother in law, Adam has an unexplainable love for all things Nicholas Cage. My buddy Dave drinks PBR because it is both cost effective and amusing. He also wears plaid and has a fixed gear bicycle, which is three strikes, so he might actually be a hipster. Pages of anecdotal examples could follow. Suffice it to say, we have become an increasingly ironic society.

Snark is a more insidious beast. It is malicious sarcasm, which makes it a generally negative quality. Sarcasm is already a social device employed to make people feel less intelligent and/or belittle things or situations. Sarcasm is a tolerable and sometimes positive quality as long as it's at least semi good-natured. Jerry Seinfeld has enjoyed a long and absurdly prosperous career built upon a strong foundation of sarcasm.

Snark is easily observed in hipsters because it is most often seen in elitist people. The social purpose of snark is a self-serving way to validate yourself. I will regularly communicate with people in a way that makes them feel less special, which increases my own feelings of specialness by comparison. I *will* be special.

Because an entire generation of people has been led to believe that they are better, unique, and more special than their peers, it's not all that surprising that these people have started acting better and smarter than everyone else. Unfortunately, many of them are not acting; they zealously believe that they stand head and shoulders above everyone else. I am not actually sure which scenario is worse.

Hipsters represent a different cultural pattern than the gothic and emo cultures. Hipsters seem to remain hipsters for much longer than members of other countercultures. Try to recall the last time you saw a member of the gothic or emo cultures older than thirty. I'm sure they exist, but in extremely small numbers and probably only come out of hiding to make shadow based predictions about upcoming seasonal weather patterns.

It's not uncommon to see hipsters in their thirties and early forties, and that number will continue to rise. Like surfers, they seem to have a long-term commitment to the culture. Unlike surfers, they don't really have a reason to continue being a part of this culture other than a lingering need to feel relevant.

What makes hipsters different is equal parts timing and tenacity. Hipster culture became popular after the Self-Esteem Movement had already altered our cultural mindset. We were all already special, so we must remain special throughout adulthood. Hipster culture reinforces feelings of specialness and uniqueness in more than one way. This has culminated in an ever evolving culture geared toward generating feelings of elitist specialness, and an ever aging population within that culture that is (perhaps desperately) clinging to the truths that were given to them as children – I am a special and unique snowflake.

Another interesting point about hipsters as a counterculture is that they seem to lack the unifying aspect of many other countercultures. Emo kids had emo music. Hippies had (and still have) jam music, festivals,

LSD, and Nitrous Oxide. Surfers have surfing. Bikers have motorcycles. Gothic people have a unifying love of gothic literature and paleness. One could argue that hipsters rally around their unyielding love of the underground, but that is too broad. Hipsters are united by a need to feel special, different, unique, and better than others. They are a counterculture that exists solely to perpetuate their self-imposed feelings of specialness.

Hiding behind walls of snark has contributed to a festering cynicism that is widespread in our society. Of this, I am more guilty than most. More often than not, I simply cannot believe that people are doing anything at all with altruistic intent. I'm the guy who assumes it will rain just because I plan to go to the beach. This oppressive pessimism has hardened into a protective barrier around us. We are impervious to the pain of a negative outcome if we are always assuming the worst.

Armoring ourselves in cynicism pairs nicely with being told you are an inherently special being. Special things do not fail. Special people do not accept negative outcomes. Even if they do, they can at least save face by being too cool to care. A flippant attitude goes a long way in proving that you, in fact, don't give a fuck about the current situation. That way you can continue to feel special, because special people are impervious to the sting of failure. Special people don't care that they failed, because they have, like, a thousand better ideas that are sure to succeed and provide them with the validation that they so desperately crave.

GENESIS

When I began researching the Self-Esteem Movement, every fiber of my being was certain that this was the work of a First (or maybe Second) Lady. I was completely unsure which, but I knew with conviction that one of them was somehow responsible for this. After all, Nancy Reagan had the D.A.R.E. program and Tipper Gore spearheaded the initiative that culminated in the parental advisory sticker. Both of which had results that were decidedly opposite of their intent. Given the almost universal failure of the Self-Esteem Movement, it was natural to assume that self-esteem was the issue de jour of some good intentioned lady living in the White House. Much to my surprise, this was not the case.

The genesis of the Self-Esteem Movement is often cited as the 1969 publication *The Psychology of Self-Esteem* written by Dr. Nathaniel Branden, in which he states that self-esteem is "the key to success in life." This work was well received and increased awareness of how a person's self-esteem may impact other areas of their life. I acknowledge the importance of this work for being one of the first to bring awareness to the subject; however, I do not cite Branden as the source of the Self-Esteem Movement that began nearly twenty years later.

In the late 1980's the California State Assembly established the Self-Esteem Task Force. The task force issued a publication in 1989 stating that self-esteem was a "vaccine" for many of the negative aspects of society including drug taking and poor academic achievement. They went on to assert that, since self-esteem is akin to vaccination, it is the responsibility of the government to provide it as they would a vaccine. This undeniably clever phrasing helped the task force to achieve the intended attention and results.

California schools began devoting time each day to teaching students ways to build their self-esteem. Schools began to give new awards to students for being a good listener, or being on time every day, or for anything else even slightly above arbitrary. Praising students regularly for *something* became a teaching requirement.

Proponents of the Self-Esteem Movement defended these actions by saying that these behaviors were not spoon feeding self-esteem, but reinforcing choices in a way that will increase positive decision making in the future. They felt that this reinforcement would help children learn how to generate feelings of positive self-worth independently in the future. From there, much like a plague, the Self-Esteem Movement spread outward in every direction, quickly infiltrating the schools and communities of America.

The man credited with creating the Self-Esteem Task Force is former California State Senator, John Vasconcellos. Prior to his becoming a senator, he was valedictorian of his class at Santa Clara University. In fact, he was always an excellent student. After brief service in the Army, he returned to California where he completed law school and became a successful lawyer.

Vasconcellos entered politics and served in the California State Assembly from 1967-1996, and then as a state senator for two terms making him the longest serving elected state official in the history of California. Because both of his positions ended due to term limitations, his record will continue to stand unless future legislation allows for longer service. During his tenure as a politician, this man did unquestionable good, but in 1986, he proposed the Self-Esteem Task force, which is all that will be discussed.

It would be hard to argue that John Vasconcellos was not a successful man. It would be hard to argue that he was not a popular man when one considers his lengthy career as an elected official. The thing I find most interesting about him is that he reports having engaged in decades of therapy to address and resolve his feelings of low self-esteem. This was his motivation to advocate for childhood self-esteem, which remains an objectively noble cause.

Vasconcellos is a man that excelled in academics, enjoyed a successful career, was objectively popular (at least in election years), and had at least some interest in helping others. He also started an initiative to increase self-esteem in children because low self-esteem was thought to have a causal relationship with low academic achievement, criminal behavior, decreased success in careers, decreased social skills, and a diminished ability to act in altruistic or empathetic ways. The man leading the charge is living, breathing evidence that contradicts all of his own points. Shockingly, nobody seemed to draw this conclusion at the time and everyone jumped on the self-esteem bandwagon.

John Vasconcellos has been quoted in defense of the Self-Esteem Movement as saying, "Kids who have a good sense of themselves and are avidly curious will learn . . . and never stop learning. All the research in the world won't change my mind about it." This is probably a true statement, the truth of which probably has very little to do with self-esteem.

What can be extrapolated from that quotation is that John Vasconcellos, having obtained (after many years) a high level of self-esteem, balks at *science* because he is special and is entitled to have his opinions and beliefs regarded as fact. He dismisses the hundreds of studies that have consistently shown no correlation between high self-esteem and academic achievement, a decrease in negative behaviors, career success, or life satisfaction as an adult. Mr. Vasconcellos, it would seem, has fallen victim to the movement he helped to pioneer. This is irony so pure and sweet I want to drizzle it over my pancakes.

Vasconcellos even thought that increased self-esteem could help balance the budget of California and the country. This is because he believed that people with higher levels of self-esteem made more money. If we increase the number of people with high self-esteem, we increase the amount of taxes being paid; therefore, balancing the budget just by making people feel good about themselves. I have no idea why this initiative was allowed to continue when the person spearheading the cause was making such wildly illogical statements.

Focusing on the self-esteem of children is not an idea that needlessly sprang from the ether. Like most movements, there were underlying factors at play that warranted action. In this case, it is best to look at the people driving the initiative, and examine their collective childhood. The Self-Esteem Movement is in many ways a natural reaction to the style of parenting that was widely utilized by the parents of the Baby Boomers.

I am the first member of my paternal family to have attended college. This is not entirely due to the intellectual capabilities of my father's family, but was largely a product of the parenting style adopted by my paternal grandparents. As has been mentioned, my grandfather was the proprietor of a small grocery store and a farmer. He was a warm and loving man to his grandchildren. I have been told he was not unkind to his children, but was always frank with them, sometimes to their detriment.

When my father expressed interest in attending college after high school, the response from my grandparents was less than supportive. My grandfather saw no pragmatic benefit of paying for his children to attend a university; after all, he had forged a decent living using nothing but hard work and force of will. There was also the matter of the farm and store that would need to be taken over by at least some of the children, neither of which required a college education. My father never attended college, and seemed to have a permanent chip on his shoulder because of it.

One can only assume that there are millions of stories similar to this one involving young Boomers being treated without regard to self-esteem. These are the moments burned into our memory. The 'when I have kids I will never do (insert whatever it is your parent just did here)' promises we make to our future children and ourselves. A generation of these experiences can lead to collectively low self-esteem. The Baby Boomers took notice of this, and many independently decided to build self-esteem in their children since it represents the opposite of the parenting they experienced.

Cultural reactions are usually impulsive and tend to have a pendulum like quality. Once it has been set in motion, it swings past the middle ground and into the opposite extreme. The Self-Esteem Movement is at the end of the swing, where the pendulum seemed to get stuck, at least for a while. Growing cultural unrest with young people who feel entitled to success and happiness at all times indicates that the pendulum may have started its swing back toward the middle, where it will almost certainly bypass reason and careen toward some other reactionary movement.

Economics factored heavily into the parenting styles that were popular when the Baby Boomers were still babies. Inflation had yet to alter the standard of living in any significant way. In 1978, minimum wage was $2.65 per hour. Adjusted for inflation that is $9.49, approximately 30% higher than current minimum wage. My main rational for choosing 1978 is because many of the parents of my generation were attending high school, or beginning their adult lives during this time. The rest of the reasoning for 1978 and the argument that follows is entirely because of *Smokey and the Bandit*. Please, bear with me.

A new Pontiac Trans-Am cost $5,799.00 in 1978, which is $20,768.25 after adjusted for inflation. Because of the popularity of Burt Reynolds's car (and mustache) in the film, 1978 represents and remains one of the most popular years of the Trans-Am. I assume that there was an increase in price because of this, making this an expensive choice of car for the time. The closest modern equivalent is a Chevrolet Camaro SS, which currently retails anywhere between $35,000 and $45,000. Yes, I am painfully aware of how white trash that example is, that's why there was a warning.

I am not suggesting that teenagers were able to purchase new cars with the earnings from their part-time, minimum wage jobs in the seventies; however, the relative price of cars was so much lower, that very nice used cars were well within their reach. Because freedom of movement is such a motivating factor for teenagers, it made sense to encourage fiscal responsibility and work ethic by making teenagers buy their own cars. The fringe benefit for parents is that they could use that money to take a vacation or buy themselves a new car instead of worrying about their child's transportation.

Jobs for unskilled teenagers were relatively easy to come by, so teens were generally expected to get a job in order to earn money for the things they wanted and needed. My father started helping out on the family farm in his pre-teen years to earn money for school clothes and new hunting equipment. He continued to work on the farm and held a variety of other jobs as a teenager. He was able to buy several cars in his teens and early twenties without financing or any degree of financial assistance. Some of his more impressive selections were a couple of late sixties big block Chevelles, an early seventies Barracuda, and a 1967 Camaro, which I choose to mention to further contextualize my fondness for muscle cars and white trash revelry of all sorts.

My mother drove a school bus when she was in high school, which despite being wildly irresponsible on the part of the school system, earned her enough money to buy a car. She bought an MG, which makes me thankful that my father taught me about what constitutes a good car. My Nana drove a new Lincoln at the time, because she didn't have to worry about buying a car for my mother. This represented the norm in the seventies, because it was realistic and feasible.

The parents of my generation again decided to take an opposite approach in many cases. Not unusually, the pendulum of indulgence swung too far in the opposite direction. They may have resented their parents for forcing them to work and buy their own goods. Their kids won't have to work. Their kids won't resent them. In fact, not only will their kids not work, they will give their kids much more than their parents ever gave them. Their kids will love them, one iPad, Xbox and BMW at a time.

Reactionary parenting styles combined with the government of California taking an interest in self-esteem cobbled together the monstrosity that would become the Self-Esteem Movement. The parents of my generation looked back on their childhood and decided to cast blame on the harsher parenting style of the day. The natural impulse was to be warmer, more indulgent parents. Since Americans aren't exactly known for their ability to do anything in moderation, we dove headfirst into the Self-Esteem Movement, creating a generation of increasingly self-centered and entitled people, but at least they have high self-esteem.

EDUCATIONAL ESTEEM

In the future, education during this era will be defined by the Self-Esteem Movement. Self-esteem has been funneled down the throats of children from the time they walk into their first classroom. Predictably, any sort of factual data continues to show that education has been significantly damaged by the onslaught of self-esteem. When reported individually, many of these numbers seem like very positive things. Taken as a whole however, it's easy to recognize some disturbing trends and identify some of the more insidious effects of the Self-Esteem Movement.

Once upon a time, there was this thing called a bell curve. It looked something like this:

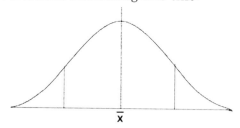

The bell curve represents a distribution of scores across people. A few people fail, a few people do exceedingly well, and the majority of the people fall somewhere in between. This held true for standardized tests as well as grades. Education has changed in the past twenty years in such a way that the bell curve no longer applies to grades. Studies have found that significantly more A's and B's are being assigned with fewer F's and D's. The result is a negatively skewed curve in which the average is actually well above average.

According to the Department of Education, grade point average (GPA) has increased nationally by an average of .32 from 1990-2009. This statistic looks great when observed in a vacuum. An overall increase in our national GPA suggests that the American education system is a well-oiled machine, and our children are becoming more intelligent, which would be wonderful, if only it were true.

While subjective measures of performance like GPA have increased, standardized measures of intelligence and achievement have remained relatively stable. Average IQ continues to be around 100. SAT scores have hovered around 500 for reading and 510 for math. ACT scores consistently average 21. These scores have been stable for decades, and will likely remain stable for decades to come. Additionally, they all (more or less) arrange themselves nicely into a bell curve. So, no, the children of America are not getting smarter. They are staying pretty much the same, but being told they are smarter by grade inflation.

What is grade inflation? Why, I'm so glad you've asked. Grade inflation is exactly what it sounds like, it's an enormous problem. Quality of work remains stable, while grades increase. It is the product of adults that are afraid to damage the self-esteem of children, so they lie to them. Students (and parents) are being pandered to by school systems across the country.

Vanguard High School, in Florida recently had a graduating class with twenty-five valedictorians, all of whom had 5.0 GPAs. Twenty-five students who got straight A's throughout high school, including college and honors courses. Vanguard chooses to calculate class rank based entirely on GPA, which probably accounts for at least a dozen of their valedictorians, but it cannot explain the entirety of the situation.

The Self-Esteem Movement permeated the values of Vanguard High School. Instead of calculating rank based on numeric grades to determine which student had actually achieved the highest overall grades, they chose to have a twenty-five way tie. The only motivating factor behind this decision had to be self-esteem. The other students worked so hard, they might feel badly about themselves if they aren't valedictorian as well. I assume the rest of the graduates tied for salutatorian. Self-esteem aside, the fact that twenty-five students finished high school without ever making a B is reason enough to discuss this issue. Either Ocala, Florida is a breeding ground for geniuses (it's not), or this is easily documented evidence of grade inflation.

I suppose this was an inevitable outcome. If everybody gets a trophy during basketball season, then giving everyone A's and B's during report card season only seems fair. The result of this is intelligent students having their learning experience sullied. I think that this is even worse than handing out trophies during sports. At least in sports, the athletic kids can observe and measure ways in which they are better at sports than their peers. Intelligent kids can do the same, but it's a much more ambiguous scenario for them – it's hard to measure achievement if everyone just gets an A.

Handing out academic praise semi-arbitrarily to all students decreases motivation to achieve. If doing *anything* warrants praise from the teachers and administrators, then there is little motivation to actually make an effort. I am atrociously guilty of this. I was a horrendously lazy student. I once wrote a lengthy analysis of the relationship between *The Lord of the Rings* trilogy and Norse mythology for my senior English class. To this day I have never read The Lord of the Rings trilogy, and couldn't be bothered to read them all just for one paper. I cobbled the whole thing together using research and bullshit, and got an A. My most sincere apologies to Mrs. Abadia. School seemed laughably easy, and they were handing out A's by the time I was high school. There was simply no motivation for me to study or exert myself when I could coast by with A's and B's.

The culture of education in America at the time did me a tremendous disservice. Had there been some motivation to apply myself throughout high school, I might have achieved something great or impressive. Instead, I put in minimal effort because that was all that was reinforced. Many of my peers did the same. We are a generation of wasted potential because we were never consistently encouraged to apply ourselves as students. For me, this resulted in a relatively lax work ethic in college, where I chose to pursue a fascinating and somewhat easy degree path with few viable career options associated with it.

Students feel entitled to high grades, as if their very tangible specialness is deserving of A's without effort. There has been a fundamental shift in the way that most students respond to grades. They receive high marks with little evidence of pride. They react to low grades with frustration, just as they always have. The difference is that students are no longer frustrated with themselves when they earn a low grade, that frustration is directed toward teachers when they are given a low grade, the operative words here being 'earn' and 'given.'

Entitlement has perpetuated a culture in which students are allowed to have an external locus of control. Meaning that students are allowed to take credit for the positive aspects of their existence, and blame external factors for the negative aspects. Grade inflation creates students that demand high grades as a validation of their feelings of specialness. They are certain of their intelligence and will not let low grades tell them otherwise, no matter how accurate they may be.

I have been questioned by numerous students on numerous occasions about low grades. These are usually demanding emails that say something to the effect of 'why did you take so many points off my assignment.' That would be the entirety of the email in many cases, no subject, no salutation, no regard for grammar, and no identifying information other than an email address.

Many of these students had gotten a B. I have explained to a relatively disheartening number of students that a college course should not be easy, will not be graded softly, and that a B is by no means a bad grade.

Students have been conditioned to believe that they deserve nothing less than high grades regardless of their effort, or the difficulty level of the course. Failing a course is out of the question, as it invalidates their feelings of intelligence and specialness. Failing represents an unacceptable outcome, since we no longer do things unless they result in success.

A staggering number of students have been suing universities for 'useless degrees.' Having spent four years of my life working toward a bachelor's degree in psychology, I admit that I am not entirely against this idea. However, students pursuing degrees of certain types have some knowledge that a bachelor's degree is no longer sufficient in their field. My entire psychology program was reminded of this more than once, and we were frequently encouraged to consider graduate school and/or PhD programs. The students who choose to sue universities seem to be doing so not because their degree is particularly useless, but because it isn't particularly lucrative. Another example of young people having an obstinately external locus of control – the university is (financially) responsible for their choice of major and their unwillingness to consider further education.

A specific (and personally abhorrent) example of a student suing a university is the case of Megan Thode, formerly of Lehigh University. Ms. Thode was enrolled in her second and final year of a Masters of Counseling and Human Development program at Lehigh University in 2009. She received a C+ in her fieldwork (internship) course, which did not meet the B grade requirement for her to be promoted to the next level of courses. Her professors state that she was enrolled in a supplemental internship course midway through the semester to help her further develop her counseling skills, so the unfavorable outcome of the course should not have been a surprise. Ultimately, they felt that she was not ready to move on, and assigned a grade C+, meaning she would have to retake the course before being eligible to finish the program.

Instead of working with her professors to reflect on areas of growth and developing the necessary skills to become a competent and successful therapist, Thode transferred to a human development master's program, which she ultimately completed. She then sued the university for "denying her a career" and sought $1.3 million in damages, representing her estimation of lifetime loss in earning potential due to her inability to complete her original program and become a therapist.

I assume that Thode would have also demanded reimbursement for tuition had she not attended Lehigh free of charge because her father was a professor at the university. Looking a gift horse in the mouth, indeed. Instead of taking ownership of her shortcomings, she went on the assault and blamed the program and her professors for her failure. Poor form from an aspiring therapist, a profession that trades on self-awareness.

Whole language was another concept popularized in the nineties. It was not a direct product of the Self-Esteem Movement, but was certainly in line with its values, which only encouraged it to exist far longer than it rightfully should have. Whole language encouraged phonetics by allowing children to sound out and spell words in whatever way they saw fit. As long as it made sense to the student, then it was correct.

I am the product of a school that adopted the whole language approach. I suppose that somewhere along the line, a teacher in a higher grade was supposed to teach us things like spelling and grammar, but that never really happened. Because of whole language I am, and will always be, horrible at spelling. When combined with growing up in the rural South, it's nothing short of amazing that I can write a coherent sentence at all. Advocates for whole language (perhaps unintentionally) chose the emotions and self-esteem of children over accurately teaching fundamental skills that they will need for the rest of their lives.

Since making self-esteem the primary focus of parenting and education, there have been vocal opponents of retention. Their concern is that the potential emotional damage done to students who are required to repeat a grade outweighs any academic implications of promoting them to the next grade. They do not bother with discussion of the potential decrease in self-esteem brought on by promoting a student into an environment where they are not capable of mastering the material at the same rate as their peers. Emotion trumps knowledge yet again.

A study conducted on 6th grade students in 2001 found that students ranked failing a grade as the most stressful event that could happen to them. The death of a parent and going blind were ranked second and third, respectively. Despite the fact that middle school children lack the same understanding of death that adults have, this is absurd. Few people would expect failing a grade to rank higher than the death of a parent.

The cultural mindset apparent in these results is that failing a grade is worse because it is something that does not happen to everyone. Everyone has parents, and everyone's parents will die. It is a universal experience. Failing a grade is more idiosyncratic and contradicts every other message the children of the Self-Esteem Movement have been given. Very suddenly, everything true could potentially be false. Failing a grade means you might not be special. You might not even be *average*, and that is completely impossible.

Dropout rates are worth mentioning, but not in detail. The National Center for Education Statistics show national dropout rates decreased from 12.1% in 1990 to 7.4% in 2010. Any number of factors may have contributed to this decrease. Perhaps increased focus on self-esteem has created students that are confident and motivated to complete school. The more likely scenario probably has more to do with grade inflation. Successful students are less likely to drop out, and the education system has started arbitrarily handing out success.

Inflated levels of achievement and self-esteem have apparently encouraged students to stay in school, which is an objectively good thing. The ends almost justify the means, but the implications of this spoon fed success are the more concerning factor. Students given achievement believe that they are achieving, creating adults who enter the work force without understanding that achievement usually requires some degree of effort.

Since 1966, the American Freshman Survey has polled rising college freshman to rate themselves against their peers on a variety of areas. Areas of inquiry include drive to achieve, leadership ability, intellectual self-confidence, social self-confidence, writing ability, mathematics, understanding others, and cooperation. Tracking the results of the surveys over the past four decades shows that an increasing number of students are ranking themselves as 'above average' on categories related to individual achievement. Categories that are less individual (cooperation, spiritualty, understanding others, etc.) have either remained stable or slightly decreased. The Self-Esteem Movement has resulted in measurably increased confidence that is not justified by anything factual. Conversely, a similar study in Asia has found stability in rankings despite increasing achievement in students. This is why my daughter will probably be learning Mandarin as a preemptive measure.

Fugazi success generates confidence that is very real. Generation Y and the Millennials have had self-esteem sewn into every fiber of their being. We have been told with conviction that we are special creatures.

A large portion of this came from the people responsible for our education. The education system has allowed us to believe that we are much more intelligent than we actually are, creating an entire generation of people who are extremely confident and extremely ignorant.

Americans are at the peak of their obnoxiousness and self-esteem's infiltration of the education system is one of the major culprits. Factor in the number of people who consider browsing Wikipedia a sufficient method of gaining expertise on a subject, and the number of truly intelligent people will continue to decline as the number of people who believe they are intelligent will continue to rise. Overly confident people operating with limited knowledge will generally react aggressively when their worldview is challenged by things like fact or reason.

SWANSONIAN ETHICS

Ron Swanson, of *Parks and Recreation*, is the greatest character currently on American television. Ron Swanson probably hates the Self-Esteem Movement. He probably thinks we have ruined children, and people in general. His character is the antithesis of the Self-Esteem Movement. He is everything that Michael Scott, formerly of Dunder Mifflin Paper Company and *The Office*, is not.

Ron Swanson can be aptly described as a 'man's man,' portrayed as a stoic and unwavering figure. He builds what he needs, hunts and kills things to eat, grows thoroughly impressive mustaches, and has a totalitarian outlook that espouses that no one is entitled to any more or less than anyone else. There is a quiet confidence about his character that exudes authenticity. He self identifies as a Libertarian and holds individual rights above all else. Ron Swanson believes that we are all entitled to the pursuit of happiness as Americans. Entitled not to happiness itself, but to the pursuit of it.

Swanson requires no external validation whatsoever. His level of self-esteem remains stable, because it is a construct of his own achievements and abilities. Nobody told the younger, less mustachioed Ron Swanson that he was special without purpose. He earned his confidence through achievement, making it genuine and much stronger than the arrogance manufactured by the Self-Esteem Movement.

Ron Swanson refuses to fall victim to the many shortcuts encouraged by the pushers of self-esteem. He values work, pragmatism, and practice; but more than these, he values ownership of both success and failure. Instead of wishing a colleague and friend luck in his future endeavor, he chooses to say, "I would wish you luck, but I believe that luck is a concept invented by the weak to explain their failures."

Blaming luck is a crutch that can help you maintain the delicate specialness that has been carefully crafted over the course of your youth and adolescence. If bad luck is not to blame, then poor performance, lack of effort, or a variety of other factors might be culpable, all of which mean that you might not be as great as you thought you were. Ron Swanson dismisses this as complete hogwash. He handles success like a man, and accepts his failures and shortcomings in like fashion.

Taking a page (the only page, actually) from Swanson's own scouting handbook, "Be a man." That is his message to youth and floundering twenty-somethings on *Parks and Rec*, and would be his advice given to their real life counterparts. Refuse shortcuts. Take credit for success and failure, the positive and the negative. It's the only way to grow and become a better human being, which was the alleged goal of this whole self-esteem business in the first place.

Swanson is not without faults of his own. He has an unhealthy and volatile relationship with both of his ex-wives. There is evidence to suggest some unhealthy attachment to his mother as well. He is often reclusive, militantly private, and demonstrates significant difficulty with interpersonal relationships outside of a select group of people.

Instead of ignoring or excusing these aspects of his existence, Swanson does the most un-snowflake thing possible; he owns them. Ron acknowledges areas in which he needs to improve, and because of this, he actively works toward bettering himself. During the progression of the show, we see him become close with other characters, establish a successful marriage, and become a competent and loving father.

Despite being too old to have been a product of the Self-Esteem Movement, Michael Scott displays many of the negative outcomes associated with it. In pretty much every factual way, Michael Scott and Ron Swanson are opposites. Michael Scott cannot build things, would not kill things, grows inferior facial hair, and (mostly unintentionally) holds himself in higher regard than others. Regardless of their fundamental differences, both men would certainly rate themselves highly in confidence, intelligence, and achievement.

Michael Scott believes that he is confident. He believes that he is special and intelligent. He carries himself in this way, but his frailty becomes evident when these beliefs are challenged. This is most easily observed in the first few seasons of *The Office*, before they really started humanizing the characters. Michael is portrayed as having very shallow confidence that covers extremely deep feelings of insecurity. He consistently seeks external validation and approval, and will break down when he does not receive it. The absence of genuineness is why his self-image is so fragile. Scott's lack of authenticity is what makes his character so grating. Many people would argue that he is not a particularly unlikeable character. These people are wrong. If Michael Scott were a real person, and really your boss, you would probably hate him.

One illustrative scene shows a corporate disciplinary meeting in which he and salesman Dwight Schrute are seated across from two corporate employees. Michael haplessly defends the actions of his employee during the initial phases of the meeting. Once it becomes apparent that corporate will win this argument, Michael stands up, takes a seat at the other side of the table, and begins to reprimand Dwight. He needed to be on the winning side of the argument with such ferocity that he changed his argument nearly mid-sentence. He needs to be on the (literal) winning side in order to feel validated. He no longer feels special if he is wrong.

The ending of another episode shows Michael in one of the show's 'confessional' scenes. Seemingly, the fictional 'producers' of the show asked him if he needed to be liked by others. His response was "Do I need to be liked? Absolutely not. I like to be liked. I enjoy being liked. I have to be liked. But it's not like this, compulsive, need to be liked. Like my need to be praised."

Michael Scott requires praise and admiration. It's not something nice to have, it is a requirement for his continued existence. Without regular praise, he has no evidence to reinforce the idea that he is special. Logically this is because he is not particularly special. He has no talents to speak of, which include the interests he pursues throughout the course of his tenure as regional manager. In fact, the show generally portrays him as less intelligent, less confident, and less socially adept than his coworkers.

Ron Swanson is a talented woodworker and outdoorsman. Other than that, he is not a particularly special person. The difference between these two men is that Ron Swanson doesn't care if he is special, and he certainly doesn't concern himself with the opinion of others. Michael Scott, on the other hand, would spend days ruminating about ways to prove his specialness to you. This is the difference in manufactured confidence and self-esteem born of authenticity.

Every child infused with unwarranted levels of self-esteem and confidence is at risk of becoming an adult like Michael Scott, insecure and anxious people who need excessive amounts of praise just to function on a daily basis. Michael is a fitting metaphor because he is not without redeeming qualities. He is often shown as kind and loving, and very obviously cares about his 'work family.' Without the façade of confidence that he feels is necessary, he would be a very likeable character. It is not my intention to suggest that increased self-esteem creates people who are terrible or unlikeable by default. My assertion is that inflated self-esteem generates qualities in adults that make it harder to find and appreciate the genuine aspects of their personality.

In the first few weeks of employment with a large company, I found myself in a large conference room for a quarterly staff meeting. The only item on the agenda that I can recall is discussion of an employee satisfaction survey that had been issued by the management team prior to my employment. Management was pleased with the overall results of the survey, but found that they rated low on an item measuring the degree to which staff members felt recognized or appreciated by their supervisors each day.

Unfortunately, this is a common problem. The most consistently cited complaint about the American workplace is that employees do not feel appreciated. The fact that this item ranks consistently low across settings indicates that we have come to expect regular commendations. Like Michael Scott, we have become a workforce that cannot operate without consistent praise.

Management handled this gracefully and pointed out that they will increase recognition efforts without saturating employees with praise. Simply doing your does not warrant someone going out of their way to praise you. Special recognition should be reserved for instances of exceptional performance. Paychecks already do a pretty amazing job of reinforcing a person's willingness to show up and adequately fulfill their job duties.

Without constant reinforcement and/or praise, we are unable or unwilling to perform up to our potential.

Workers may freeze up without reinforcement, and use that lack of praise to assume they are not doing a good job. They may become so anxious about doing a bad job that they forget to do their job at all.

Positions that involve working independently have become increasingly difficult for workers in our society. People in these positions often find that they are not gratifying or fulfilling, and usually cite feeling isolated as the reason for this. I think the more honest answer is that there are fewer opportunities to be praised and be validated by supervisors. Teaching children self-esteem to such a high degree reduces their ability to self-soothe because they will continue to seek outside validation, resulting in less independent adults. The more dependent the work force, the less innovation and development will occur.

The Self-Esteem Movement spawned a culture that rains down praise on children for any and every reason. Children become accustomed to this constant reinforcement ensuring them of their specialness, uniqueness, intelligence, etc. Once those children reach adulthood and enter the work force, they continue to expect consistent validation. They need to be praised, regardless of their efforts, to maintain their motivation to do the bare minimum, a generation of workers much more Scott than Swanson.

SOUTH BY SOUTHEAST

I was born in the South. With any luck, I will die in the South and my bones will be laid to rest beside those of family. Tar Heel born and Tar Heel bred, indeed. When presented with any number of situations, both hypothetical and real, I often find myself considering what impact my Southern heritage has on my outlook, values, and decision making.

While I have never been one to wave around a Confederate flag, my blinding love of being Southern makes it impossible to write about my homeland in anything but the most biased of ways. Consider this a preemptive acknowledgement and dismissal of any and all criticisms directed toward this particular essay.

Many times in the infancy of the ideas that would become this book, I assumed that my rural upbringing had sheltered me from the Self-Esteem Movement. While this remains true, I think that the culture of my region itself is more responsible than the decidedly rural place where I spent my youth. After all, there are rural areas across the country that are infinitely more progressive than even the most liberal areas of the South.

The South rebelled, was conquered, and left to rebuild itself from the (literal) ashes. The rebellion was snuffed out, and for the better part of two centuries, the South has been looked down upon as the rebels who might have been. In a strange way, this is the essence of the fierce pride that is associated with the very act of being Southern. There is a tenacity that comes from being the underdog.

While the northern states focused on industrialization, their southern brethren writhed in poverty, trying desperately to rebuild the agrarian aristocracy that was so very ineffective without slavery. Because the land in the southern United States was especially fertile, farming was a sound (and potentially lucrative) profession. Once slavery ended, this was no longer the case, but the infrastructure of the South (even prior to the war) was not equipped to become an industrialized society. As a region, it had always existed as a subsidiary of the northern states. There were no real cities, only ports and farms, because that is what was encouraged during the settlement of America. The South existed in a way not unlike that of a colony.

The South has remained more sparsely populated and less affluent than many other areas of the country. Most of its collars are blue. The region could simply never catch up to the rest of the country after the Civil War. It remains a place of farms and fishing businesses passed down through generations. It remains a place of tradition and pride.

The county where I grew up has a population density of less than 50 people per square mile, which will likely be true for the foreseeable future. It's not difficult to find someone there who has never seen a building with more than three floors. Like most markedly rural places, it's also quite poor. It is this seemingly negative combination of poor and rural that has shielded many Southern children from the more obviously negative impacts of the Self-Esteem Movement. This is not to say that the South has been unaffected; rather that the Self-Esteem Movement has had significantly less ability to influence the region because of these factors.

Citizens of rural communities have much less to occupy their time than their counterparts in cities and suburbs. Southerners are known for being slow of both speech and action, largely because there is no real incentive to act with haste. Depending on your view, this is either obnoxious or endearing. When there is little to occupy free time, people begin to focus on the things available to them with great interest. In many cases, these things include manners and respect. Children of the South have traditionally been taught to open doors, say 'please' and 'thank you', and use 'mam' and 'sir.' Disrespect is easily noticed and discouraged, simply because there is often naught to do other than talk and listen, which is how the Southern people developed their predilection for telling stories that are much longer than they rightfully should be.

By teaching children respect, it teaches them that there is a hierarchy to things. You are expected to show respect to your elders and superiors. You may be shown respect in return, but are reminded that this is a courtesy and should be viewed as such. Despite the ever dwindling number of Southern children taught respect in a traditional sense, this cultural value has bolstered children against easily developing a sense of unique specialness that transcends all other beings, and entitlement to the respect and admiration of everyone.

In addition to respect, Southern culture upholds humility as one of its core values. In *House of Cards*, Frank Underwood points out that humility is a form of pride in the South. You generate self-worth by accomplishing things, but remaining humble in an almost self-deprecating kind of way. Upholding and reinforcing humility to this degree directly contradicts many of the fundamental values of the Self-Esteem Movement.

Traditional Southern values expect a person to use what talents are afforded to him, but only in a moral way that doesn't upset or offend their community, or at least this is the rosy underpinnings of the value. As Underwood demonstrates, many shrewd folks readily exploit this humility. However, the sense that this is a community value transcends examples of individual malice. As a region, the South tends to have a greater sense of community, and with that comes increased awareness of how actions affect other people. A strong sense of community counteracts the viciously individual teachings of the Self-Esteem Movement.

The less affluent the family, the less likely they are able to spend frivolously on their children. The standard of living in the South is less than that of other regions. Many families support themselves with 'blue collar' jobs and live from one paycheck to the next. These families are not in a position to shower their children with the newest and most expensive of consumer goods, and there is no better defense against consumerist entitlement than the inability to provide it.

Children of these families learn to internalize the value of work and earning possessions out of necessity. There are no new cars or computers to make up for a perceived detriment in self-esteem. Abraham Maslow's hierarchy of needs dictates that basic physiological needs must be satisfied well before focusing on self-esteem. As with members of older generations, parents are generally too concerned with providing necessities for their family to spend time dissecting the self-esteem of their children.

The South has been impacted by the Self-Esteem Movement to a lesser degree than some other regions. Mind you, this was not an intentional outcome, and does not make the South better than any other region (even though I will always subjectively believe it is). It is a function of a region that is rural, generally poor, and the cultural mindset that permeated the people of the South in the aftermath of the Civil War.

If the South is old, rural, and poor, then the northeastern United States is a natural foil of old, urban, and affluent. While the South did its best to recover from the Civil War, the rest of the country busied themselves with industrializing and building cities. It developed, industrialized, and urbanized well before the rest of America. As a result, there are a higher percentage of white collars in the northeast. It is home to the oldest and most highly regarded Ivy League universities in the country. It's what people in the South call 'fancy.'

Where respect and honor are highly valued in Southern culture, the culture of the northeast has traditionally upheld wealth, power, and prestige. Cities have always been a more expensive place to live, especially when space is limited and demand is high. This makes living extravagantly in a city more expensive still. The higher population density of cities itself is predictive of increased numbers of wealthy people. In order to appear well to do one must spend extravagant sums of money when living in a city. This created the cultural norms that socialites in most cities continue to live by. The upper crust of Manhattan spend absurd amounts of money to live in lavish penthouses, maintain estates in the Hamptons, host fund raisers, be seen in the most exclusive restaurants, and collect the newest art from the most pretentious artists that Brooklyn has to offer.

Middle and upper-middle class people in the northeast, living in the exponentially expanding suburbs that connect the cities like a slowly encroaching fungus, observe, and are influenced by, the behavior of socialites in their nearest city. They see how differently these people are treated because their coffers are full to bursting (or so they would have you believe) and want to experience that treatment as well.

Like many poor families in other parts of the county, these suburban families dance precariously from one paycheck to the next as well. The difference is that they are attempting to emulate the extravagance of the 1%. They buy sprawling McMansions, drive a German sedan in some shade of silver or gray, enroll their children in the most exclusive and/or popular school, and do anything else within their power to ensure that everyone can observe how well they are doing financially. They feel compelled to maintain a lifestyle at least at the top of their means in order to feel successful, and their children are watching.

The children of the yuppie suburban family learn to demand the popular clothes, the newest phones and tablets, extravagant birthday parties, and new cars. They seem to internalize the value that friendship and socialization are contests to be won with material goods. Power and hierarchy are determined by possession. Parents will provide a new car to show all the other families that they too can afford to show their children the financial worth of their love. These are the families that take their big vacation each year even if it means missing a mortgage payment or two.

Parents in these family systems internalized a correlation between material success and feelings of self-worth. This value passes to their children via observation of their parents' reckless consumerism. Undoubtedly, this generates higher levels of entitlement in these children. They are entitled to the newest and best of everything as soon as they are aware of it. The materialistic battle for supremacy that permeates many of these communities leads to children who seek out validation of their self-worth through possession. People in the South are often generating worth through humility, whereas outward materialism generates esteem in the cities and suburbs of the Northeast.

Even though suburbanites are not as affluent as the upper crust of the cities, their earnings are usually sufficient to provide their children with instantaneous access to many of the frivolous things they want. Making their children wait may cause them to experience negative emotions and decrease their self-esteem. Since this is unacceptable, they jump to meet the wants of their children whenever possible. These are the parents who pay double or triple the cost of the newest gaming console to ensure that their child has one waiting under the tree at Christmas that year. These are the children who turn into despondent adults who cannot understand why they aren't immediately handed anything they want from society. I am Trey's complete lack of surprise.

Suburban families are no longer at the bottom of Maslow's hierarchy of needs. Basic physiological needs are not a concern, meaning that increased focus is given to higher order needs such as feeling loved, belonging, and self-worth. Because of this, suburban parents often find themselves fretting over self-esteem.

Does their child have enough? Do *they* have enough? Would having a bigger house or nicer car help them feel better than they do now? Could that house save their faltering marriage? Would it increase the self-esteem of their children? They have an obligation to do anything to increase their children's self-worth since society has assured them that the only way to guarantee success for their children is infuse them with sociopathic levels of self-esteem.

Parents also have a tendency to build clout in the 'burbs with the achievements of their children, usually in academics or athletics. If their child is no longer at the top of his or her class, the parents are no longer able to boast. They can't be bothered to foster strong study habits in their children, so they often blame the school. This only serves as further reinforcement of the entitlement of their children, who now believe that they are entitled to good grades regardless of their teacher's thoughts on the matter.

Legal troubles as adolescents are usually blamed on outside factors, paid off, or otherwise swept under the rug. Parents are unable to feel of greater worth than their peers if their child has been convicted of a crime. Children are learning that they can act in whatever way they choose regardless of consequences. They are objectively better than most other people because the rules do not apply to them in the same ways. Parents are conditioning them to have an external locus of control by casting blame on everything but their children when their children fall short of societal expectations.

While vacationing in Florida in 2013, former New England Patriot, Bryan Holloway's New York home was broken into by a group of local teenagers. The teens knew he was away and decided to throw a massive party in his absence. Three hundred kids destroyed that house in Spartan-like fashion. Walls were spray-painted and riddled with holes, most of the carpets were ruined, and memorabilia was stolen or defaced. Approximately $20,000 of damage was done by the party. Holloway was able to collect 170 Tweets, Facebook posts, and Instagram pictures of the party and its attendees. He recognized some of the faces, implying that many in attendance were upper class kids that lived in his neighborhood.

Holloway initially decided not to press any charges and put out an open invitation to the teens who attended the party and their families to help clean up his house. When only one person who had attended the party bothered to show up, Holloway created a website to raise awareness about teenage drinking and drug use. He populated his website using social media posts made by the partygoers. Instead of acknowledging that their children might have some culpability in the matter, parents became angry and a number of them threatened to sue Holloway for putting their children's statements and pictures on the internet. Since everything put onto social media sites is public domain, Holloway politely reminded them that they could eat a dick and should probably reassess their priorities if they were upset with him and not their children.

After a time, Holloway gave up the high road and decided to press charges on some of the teens who had participated in the destruction of his home. Since nothing else had garnered any sort of positive response, he took legal action in an effort to prevent something like this from happening again. In an interview, he simply said, "parents need to step up and go old school." I am inclined to agree with him.

The parents in this scenario chose to ignore any-thing that might implicate their children. They refused to hold them accountable for their actions, because means they must hold themselves accountable for producing children that would engage in something like this. If they admit that their children are wrong, then they might not be special. If their child is not special, they cannot use their child's glowing specialness to bolster their own feelings of worth. Like so many semi-affluent parents living in semi-affluent suburbs, they choose to bury their head in the sand and take comfort in oblivion.

In stark contrast, a former college roommate of mine did something similar when he was in high school, with a decidedly different outcome. He and a few friends broke into an unoccupied beach house in the Outer Banks of North Carolina, where they decided to stay overnight and drink whatever booze they could find. They were all arrested and charged with breaking and entering, trespassing, and underage drinking.

None of their parents came to their rescue beyond bailing them out of jail, and a few spent a few nights in holding cells before being retrieved. Court dates were scheduled and lawyers procured. The only reason that they were not tried for these crimes was because the arresting officer was dismissed of duty for some un-known unscrupulous activities, meaning that all of his pending cases were immediately dismissed.

These kids were from a semi-affluent suburb out-side of a semi-affluent city in North Carolina. I imagine that, on paper, they are very similar to the teens that

143

ruined Brian Holloway's house. Their Southern parents universally forced them to take responsibility for their actions. If nothing but region differs, then the culture of the region had some impact on how differently these similar scenarios played out.

The very idea of California has been exciting since the Europeans who 'discovered' America figured out it was there. It was the end of the New World, the final frontier. We drove westward in the name of conquest, expansion, and destiny. It was the Wild West, where anything and everything was still possible. Tales of the Gold Rush tantalized and tempted anyone who heard about it. California developed a reputation for being a place where you could show up, and become wildly rich in a matter of weeks. Generations later, that conceptual idea of California has changed very little. Even now, there is probably some young man or woman arriving in California with dreams of stardom, certain that they will be soon be showered with fame and fortune.

California has always been a place where trends were born and progressive ideas blossomed and flourished. It is where music, movies, and dreams are made. Hollywood is full of both glitz and glamour, provided that one defines those as broken dreams and crushing despair. It has always been, and will probably always be considered a new and exciting place.

California is entirely responsible for the Self-Esteem Movement. The culture of California has long been stereotyped as extremely shallow and materialistic.

In order to continue feeling special, men and women have dozens of cosmetic surgeries to maintain a youthful appearance. The old are cast aside, so value has been placed on youth. In order to continue feeling special, people must continue to be young and attractive. Failing this, you can at least try to *look* young and attractive.

Connecting the dots between the culture that has and continues to exist in California and the Self-Esteem Movement is not a difficult task. People were generating feelings of self-worth through transient means, resulting in people who had to continuously seek external validation. Presumably, children at the time internalized these behaviors as well, and appeared to have low self-esteem due to their constant need for validation. Adults who noticed this did not think to take a step back and consider cultural factors that may be contributing to this, and instead vigorously attached themselves to the cause of self-esteem.

California was ground zero for the Self-Esteem Movement. It remains the most severely impacted region. The children of the California school system received the most frequent and concentrated doses of the metaphorical vaccine (or plague, depending on your views on the subject). Children began requiring more vigorous demonstrations of their specialness. This only compounded with the external methods of validation that they learned from their culture.

I have no idea if self-esteem is being shoveled down the throats of Californian children at the same rate as it once was, but I can only assume that the ideals of the Self-Esteem Movement are so ingrained in the culture of (especially southern) California that it will be a part of their mindset for quite some time. This will continue to generate the shitty rich kids that we all love to hate so much. These vapid and terrible human beings actually represent the highest level of success that can be achieved by the Self-Esteem Movement. If the best possible outcome simultaneously generates the worst-case scenario, then something has gone horribly awry.

One of my most recent infatuations has been with Jerry Seinfeld's new pseudo-show *Comedians in Cars Getting Coffee*. The premise of the show is exactly what you think – Jerry drives a (usually awesome) car to pick up an actor/comedian friend of his and they drive to a coffee shop while their interactions are filmed.

Being a famous television personality from New York, Seinfeld divides his time between New York and Los Angeles. The show chronicles his coffee drinking extravaganzas with friends and acquaintances in both cities, which provides an interesting case study in how regional culture can influence how we interact with one another. Conversations seem to be more genuine when the show is taking place in New York. In California, there is a subtly hollow aspect present in the interactions. Most of the California based episodes are full of complimentary talk about this project or that. This holds true even when Jerry and the guest have a long-standing friendship, like with Michael Richards and Jay Leno. While these episodes are not as plastic as others,

it is still evident. Conversely, there is a tangible authenticity to many of his interactions in New York. Alec
Baldwin spends the majority of his episode trading verbal
jabs with Jerry.

Everything is constant in the show except region.
Level of affluence is equivalent. All guests are comedic
actors of some kind. The host and format are identical.
The only factor that can account for the differences in
interaction is regional culture. In Los Angeles, everyone
strives to be *somebody*. This perpetuated a culture in
which people strive to be special by being beautiful,
successful, rich, and famous. The superficial nature of
the culture generates social norms in which interactions
are full of genuine compliments given in a generally
disingenuous way.

The Midwest, which is arguably not mid or west
of anything in particular, has much in common with the
South. It has many rural places and strong blue collar
work force. Generally speaking, it is a conservative
place. It is also less affluent than other regions. Where
the two regions differ is in their cultural sense of pride.

The South has a ferocious and unwarranted
sense of cultural pride, where the Midwest lacks this.
They are very passive in this way. Midwesterners love
their home, but don't really mind if your opinion differs,
whereas many Southerners will quickly invite people to
return to the Godforsaken place whence they came if
they speak poorly about the South or its traditions.
Southerners have an unmatched ability to make an

outsider feel welcome while never letting them forget that they are a guest, and will never truly be a part of the culture. The musings that Southern culture is intentionally slow to irritate and alienate outsiders is not an entirely baseless accusation.

The Self-Esteem Movement seems to have had less effect in the Midwest than the northeastern United States or California. This is most likely due to the more conservative and traditional values of the Midwest in combination with their lower socioeconomic status. Having spent a good deal of time in the Midwest, I have observed some evidence of higher levels of infiltration of the Self-Esteem Movement than in my Southern homeland. I feel that this is because the increased sense of pride in the South upheld the traditional values that bolstered the region from the dangers of high self-esteem. The Midwest, which is a much friendlier place to outsiders, does not have this pride to reinforce their old values, which left it at least slightly more vulnerable to the effects of the Self-Esteem Movement.

It is easy to look at this argument and determine that it is much more about socioeconomic status than regional culture. Poorer, blue collar, rural places have been impacted to a lesser degree because they have less ability to focus on things like the Self-Esteem Movement. More affluent, white collar, urban places have the ability to do so and the income to monetize self-esteem to a greater degree. I concede that this is a very viable way to approach this argument, but differences in regional culture have had undeniable influence on the ways people have been affected by all manner of cultural movements, self-esteem or otherwise.

The culprit may very well be the nouveau-riche society that has taken root in the suburbs across the country, lending further credence to the argument of socioeconomic status over regional culture. However, these suburban norms developed in places like southern California and the northeastern United States. The culture of these regions were already in line with the ideals of the Self-Esteem Movement, and this culture spread into suburbs across the country, so too did the values of these communities.

As the tendrils of suburbia spread further and further, it will ceaselessly choke the uniqueness out of each of us. It saddens me to consider this point as it may very well mean that the individual charm and culture of each region will slowly wither and be cast aside. I love my home. I love the South. I know the values imparted upon me by my region have made me a better person than I might have otherwise been. My daughter will not have this experience beyond what I am able to convey to her, and that makes me saddest of all.

FAIL IS A FOUR LETTER WORD

The Self-Esteem Movement has created a culture in which failure is just about the worst thing that can happen to a person. High self-esteem was thought to bolster children against failure and make them more resilient. It was almost universally agreed upon that the higher a person's self-esteem, the better. Like most other aspects of the Self-Esteem Movement, this seems to have an inverse long term effect.

Creating baseless self-esteem in children probably works in the short term, but it also creates a false perception of what self-esteem actually is and how much of it we should have. By pushing self-esteem to such an unrealistic degree, we now assume that extremely high self-esteem is normal. The result of this is people who are operating under the assumption that they have issues with self-esteem, when they actually have an accurate and healthy self-concept.

Inputting 'self-esteem' into any search engine returns hundreds of results encompassing a wide variety of topics revolving around feelings of self-worth. Through this query one can find blogs about self-esteem, causes of low self-esteem, consequences of low self-esteem, how to increase or improve self-esteem, benefits of having high self-esteem, how to identify low self-esteem in children or yourself, books, videos, seminar courses, support groups, message boards, and occasional criticisms. Obviously, we spend a good deal of time thinking about self-esteem and having enough of it.

The way we think about self-esteem has become akin to the misconceptions about body image. The level of self-esteem encouraged culturally is the equivalent of putting size two models in magazines. Yes, there are women who are six feet tall and weigh 110 pounds, much in the same way that there are people with naturally occurring extreme levels of self-esteem. Neither represents anything approaching normalcy. We teach healthy body image to our children, but continue to perpetuate the belief that extreme levels of self-esteem not only realistic, but expected of them. By allowing this belief to exist we are setting up children to believe they have issues with self-esteem as an adult just because they are not happy and confident 100% of the time.

Quite nearly every commercial on television is peddling anti-depressant medications, all of which list symptoms that most people can easily identify with. These advertisements tend to promise improvements that most anyone would welcome. Pharmaceutical companies and the Self-Esteem Movement have caused our culture to internalize the idea that we are entitled to happiness at all times.

To be occasionally unhappy is no longer a natural experience, but a warning sign of mental illness. This mentality helps perpetuate the rampant externalization in our culture. If we are unhappy or fail, we can cast blame on illness without damaging our self-esteem. Those of us savvy enough in the ways of the snowflake may even increase feelings of self-worth by reframing our shortcomings around some imaginary struggle and triumph over adverse circumstances.

We have been conditioned to believe that we are entitled to happiness, are supposed to possess extremely high self-esteem, and be successful at all times and in all things. The pattern of disordered thinking that accompanies these values is a causal factor in the increasing number of people seeking out psychiatric treatment for depression or anxiety. Not because they are actually depressed, but because their experience is no longer congruent with their expectations of the world, and the resulting stress is enough to approximate the symptomology of these disorders.

Because we are expected to have high self-esteem at all times, we have created a society that can no longer effectively cope with failure. High self-esteem has been associated with success to such a degree that we believe that self-esteem is dependent upon success. This creates the potential for people to shut down after experiencing failure and/or refusing to attempt anything that may result in failure.

People capable of advancing society in ways we cannot even begin to fathom are currently walking the earth. Unfortunately, many of their brains have been so thoroughly washed by the Self-Esteem Movement that we will never see their ideas come to fruition due to their crippling fear of failure. If I never get my sassy robotic housekeeper and Jetson-esque automated home, I'm blaming the Self-Esteem Movement.

A childhood friend of mine is a gifted computer programmer. After high school, he attended college for computer engineering where he completed three years of the program. He dropped out and attempted to start up some sort of company, doing what, I was never quite sure. After this was unsuccessful, he moved back to our hometown and works as the accountant/IT professional for his father's company. I haven't spoken with him in years, and from what I understand he is doing well for himself, but seems to be just coasting through life. After his business venture failed, he was not willing to reen-roll and finish school, and had no interest in attempting to start another business. That was it; he took his shot and missed. He didn't dare shoot again.

A more amusing anecdotal case study is that of another gentleman that I befriended in high school. He is an absurdly intelligent person, and was awarded a full scholarship to his preferred university. Like many college freshman, he quickly realized that his time was much better spent partying than attending classes. Booze, weed, and LSD were staples of his existence. Not surprisingly, he found himself on academic probation after the first semester due to his failure to meet mini-mum requirements to maintain his scholarship.

After his grades failed to improve and a few deal-ings with the campus police, he was suspended for a year. He was eligible to return to school after his suspension was lifted, but never did. Instead, he moved back home and has been working a variety of restaurant jobs since that time. He quit using drugs entirely, but not for any reasons of morality. For a while, he had an absurdly successful side venture selling clean urine. At least failure didn't stifle his entrepreneurial spirit.

We are terrified of failure. To try and fail is far worse than doing nothing at all. Failure chips away at the self-esteem we believe that we have rightfully earned. If I fail, I might not be so special, so I will not fail, even if that means I accomplish nothing. There will always be people who have great ideas but lack the ability or initiative to implement them. Now there is another group of people who have the ability, yet are too afraid to act on their ideas, further decreasing the number of people driving the development of our culture.

Fear of failure has stifled creativity and innovation in many areas. There are those who would argue that we are currently experiencing a creative renaissance, in which people are exploring any number of new and wonderful ideas. Unfortunately, this is probably a farce. It certainly seems that way, but this is likely the product of how easy it is to expose ideas and efforts to the masses using the internet. A smaller percentage of people are taking chances, but that is hard to believe that when anyone can sell their crafts on Etsy, upload their show ideas to YouTube or Vimeo, sell their book directly through Amazon, and make sure that everyone they have ever met knows about it through Facebook, Instagram, and Twitter.

Americans have achieved record high levels of self-esteem and seem to be just as proud of themselves and their country as they ever have been. Individually, we attempt to avoid failure to prevent our feelings of pride from being challenged. We expend a great deal of effort to hide from these negative feelings. Our cultural shortcomings, however, are much harder to avoid.

Since the beginning of the Self-Esteem Movement America has been involved in three different wars. We impeached a president over a blowjob. Then we elected a president that holds the records for both highest and lowest approval ratings. The housing market almost completely collapsed. Limp Bizkit is still doing world tours. The banking and automotive industries required billions of dollars in government bailouts to continue operating. The Star Wars prequel trilogy happened. The federal government got into an argument with itself and shut down.

Since 1990, the national debt has increased by approximately thirteen trillion dollars, which is a completely made up number as far as I'm concerned. The reported unemployment rate of 7.4% is a statistic that does not account for people who are unemployed and do not qualify for unemployment benefits, meaning that the actual statistic is much, much higher.

All of these events occurred in the midst of soaring self-esteem and confidence. If there were ever a case for universally diminished self-esteem, this would be a prime contender. Instead, we find ourselves ignoring failure and mining for success in any situation. We narrow our focus until there is something to be proud of, and we desperately cling to that morsel of validation as though it was our last.

APES WITH EGO TRIPS

Existential philosophy maintains that life is an inherently meaningless endeavor. We are born, and shortly thereafter, we will die. Any greater purpose assigned to life is something that we manufacture to reduce the anxiety provoked by acknowledging that life has no real meaning. I am inclined to regard this as truth for the most part. There is not some sacred meaning of life beyond the continuation of our species, as far as I can tell.

Existentialism began in the late 19th century and generally credited to the Danish philosopher Søren Kierkegaard. He deliberately pointed out that it is not the responsibility of a culture, religion, or society to dictate meaning. We, as individuals, are responsible for our own lives and the meaning of that life. Most people find this concept completely terrifying.

Jean Paul Sarte, a 20th century French philosopher, said that all existential philosophy shares the common idea that 'existence precedes essence.' We must exist before our existence can have any meaning. This being the case, we must create our purpose independently. He believed that humans are 'condemned to be free,' that we are free to make or unmake any meaning we wish for

157

our lives. Instead of this being a feeling of liberation and freedom for humans, we recoil at the idea of having this tremendous responsibility/privilege to make our life meaningful in our own ways. I have no doubt that Sarte intentionally chose to single out humans in that statement. I have a hard time believing that any other animal experiences anxiety in relation to their ability to live life as they wish.

Humans are the only animals that appear to be uncomfortable with the very nature of our existence. Wolves probably are not preoccupied with ensuring that they have a fulfilling life or have a burning desire to leave behind a legacy beyond having as many pups as they can manage. Domesticated animals do not pretend that there is some greater meaning to existence. They sleep, eat, play, fuck, and die. They are no different than humans were before we started compulsively searching for the eternally secret and mystical purpose of life. Not all life, mind you, just human life. Most people have no issues with assigning zero meaning to the life of animals, yet feel that human existence is special, and must have some sort of unique and transcendent purpose.

Humans are a species that can no longer accept that our existence is meaningless. We need greater meaning, because we need to be special, which is one point of discussion that is not actually the result of the Self-Esteem Movement. Being too much like the other animals invalidates our collective feelings of specialness, so we have gone about much of our existence attempting to prove that humans are not animals.

The unfortunate part about all of this involves the tremendous amount of power and freedom that accompany embracing the meaninglessness of life. Not only can we choose the purpose of our own lives, we have the intellectual capacity to be aware of this and act on it. In that way, we may actually be different than other animals. We are free to captain our own ships, and joy-fully run them aground if we wish. Few of us choose to act on this knowledge because accepting this power admits that humans are not special as a species.

Humans and the other great apes diverged at the point that humans discovered fire. That's it. That is the singular thing that made us different. Had some other kind of primate discovered the usefulness of fire before our predecessors, then another kind of ape would be writing this book and I would be very contently living in a jungle somewhere.

Until the discovery of fire, the apes that would eventually become humans ate plants and sometimes raw meat. Somewhere along the line, they harnessed the power of fire, using it to provide warmth and/or as an instrument of fear against the other ape tribes. Probably by accident, one of them threw a dead animal into the fire and came to the conclusion that eating cooked meat was infinitely preferable to eating the raw meat that was occasionally available. My theory on how humans came to cook with fire is (very obviously) all conjecture on my part, but this next bit is entirely factual. The benefits of eating cooked meat are that it offers higher caloric and nutritional content, is easier to chew, and easier to digest. The result is a diet that requires less time and effort to obtain the same nutritional value.

The human brain accounts for 2% of our mass but uses 20% of our resting energy to work in the way we have become accustomed to. Gorillas have brains that are approximately one-third the size of human brains, containing one-third the neurons. In order to maintain this, most Gorillas spend approximately nine hours per day eating raw plant material. To have a brain equivalent to a human brain, they would need to eat for approximately two more hours every day. The low calorie raw plant diet of many primates prevent them from achieving a human like brain because there is simply not enough time for them to ingest the calories needed to maintain it. Even if a certain kind of ape did accomplish this, they would have time to do nothing but eat and sleep, likely rendering their increased cognitive abilities useless.

Pre-humans were spending less time grazing, and more time observing their surroundings, socializing with other proto-humans, and engaging in any number of activities that are more intellectually stimulating than foraging and eating for hours on end. More time to learn and socialize combined with an excess of nutrients allowed our brains to grow and develop beyond those of other primates. So, yes, the discovery of (cooking with) fire is essentially the only thing that sets humans apart from the other apes. We would do well to stop pretending that we aren't just (mostly) hairless apes that live in houses, have jobs, and pay taxes.

If life and the world are truly devoid of meaning (and they are), then the concept of fairness is an absurdity. Justice is not blind, and does not concern herself with achieving balance on an individual level. The world is unfair. This has always been the case, and will forever be the case. By incessantly reinforcing the idea of universal and all-encompassing specialness, the Self-Esteem Movement perpetuates the idea of fairness. Children do not lose. They are recognized with awards for almost any reason. They can be anything at all they want to be. A generation that believes they are entitled to success and immediate gratification. The unfairness of the world beyond childhood contradicts and challenges the values and beliefs of young adults who are products of the Self-Esteem Movement.

I was born an American, middle class, white male in the eighties. The advantages that come prepackaged with the demographic details of my birth are borderline vulgar. Even before I was born, it was a safe to assume that I couldn't mess up too badly without a serious drug addiction or being directly involved in the death of another person. From birth, I have had advantages that many other people will never have. That is the very definition of unfair.

Some people are born into such poor circumstances that they are likely doomed from the start. Those who do overcome horrible circumstances and demographic disadvantage usually have books and/or movies made about them, which is indicative of how rarely it actually happens. On a global scale, being born in America at all offers an insane advantage over many other places. Even the poorest children born to the most horrid teenage parents in the worst ghettos, most dilapidated trailer parks, darkest hollers, and dankest swamps in America are infinitely better off than almost any child born in Somalia.

Despite all of the advantages that accompany middle class whiteness, there are those who are born with far more advantages than even the most middle class of whiteness has to offer. Donald John Trump is an easily recognizable reminder to essentially everyone that there are those who were born with advantages well beyond what the rest of us even dare to fantasize about.

There is nothing subtle about Donald Trump, an observation that would be easy to make even if he did not christen almost every gilded building and casino he owns with his surname, or regularly spend his time firing people on television. I know very little about the Kennedy family, but have always assumed that Donald would assimilate nicely.

"The Donald," as he seems to enjoy being called, has made a fortune in real estate, mainly in New York City, where he owns 'millions of square feet' of commercial and residential space. His father, Fred Trump was born to German immigrants, and from nothing, created a large and successful real estate business in New York City focused on affordable apartment housing. At the time of his death in 1999, his estate was valued at $400 million. Rightfully, we should all be talking about Fred; but we aren't, and nobody ever does.

The Trumps were already a wealthy family by the time Donald came along. After graduating with a degree in economics in 1968, he started working for his father's real estate company, and granted control over the company in 1971. By using this company as a gateway into larger real estate business ventures, Trump has amassed a fortune of approximately three billion dollars. His annual salaries from his various companies total $60 million. In addition to this, companies that he owns, or bear his name in some fashion, have filed for corporate bankruptcy in 1991, 1992, 2004, and 2009.

The Apprentice, the reality game show hosted by Trump, premiered in 2004 and has been in production since that time. Trump was paid to criticize and 'fire' people on a business game show while at least one of his companies were in bankruptcy proceedings on two different occasions. This is only possible because the world is not a fair place. We are all dealt a hand, and The Donald's happened to be aces full of kings.

Conversely, if I found myself unable to make the payments on my home, or I owned a small business that fell deeply into debt, I would most likely lose my house and/or business. That would be it. The banks would have no mercy because there would be no real incentive for them to be merciful. They would recoup their losses as best they could and most likely never lend to me again. This is not true for people like Donald.

When some of Trump's ideas proved to be less than profitable, the company declared bankruptcy, as many companies do in that situation. The difference between bankruptcy for someone like Donald Trump, and someone like me is that bankruptcy allowed him to negotiate with the banks and benefit in the long term. He has negotiated for longer terms to pay off money, reduced debt amounts, lowered interest rates, and probably numerous other beneficial ways of which I have no knowledge or understanding.

With regard to bankruptcy, Trump has said, "We'll have the company. We'll throw it into a chapter. We'll negotiate with the banks. We'll make a fantastic deal. You know, it's like on *The Apprentice*. It's not personal. It's just business." Obviously, the concept of bankruptcy for the wealthy is much different than it is for the rest of us.

Trump is wealthy, so he was allowed to borrow a fortune. When his company could not make payments on that fortune, his lenders were at a disadvantage, because they stood to lose untold millions if they foreclosed on his properties. Taking possession of unfinished casinos in Atlantic City is apparently not the easiest way to make up losses. They stood to recoup much more money by negotiating with him and making it easier for him to pay back the monies he borrowed. When the amount of money is smaller, as it usually is, the banks are at more of an advantage because they have less to lose than the borrower. This is not the case if you happen to be insanely wealthy and can show that *you* have less to lose than a bank. It's also not fair. But that's kind of the point – the world *isn't* fair.

Without question, the idea of a fair and just world that keeps tally of your good and bad deeds is a harmful concept. Assuming that the world is a place of fairness opens the door to frequent difficulty as an adult. We begin to rely on fairness to even out things like 'bad luck,' which might be better stated as 'shit effort.' The Self-Esteem Movement has programmed us to seek out reward without effort and we have found a convenient excuse in bemoaning fairness when we fail to achieve unwarranted success with ease.

We have bastardized the concept of fairness to mean that things will be easy. Success will come without challenge. Listen carefully the next time someone begins to talk about an 'unfair' situation. More often than not, they are grumbling about a something that was more challenging than they had anticipated, and with certainty, they will be talking about a situation that did not work out in their favor. The more difficult the situation, the more likely you are to fail, which is an unacceptable outcome, so it must be unfair in some way.

The concept of fairness only seems to apply when the 'unfair' factors were not beneficial to us. When something happens to be both unfair and beneficial, we like to call it 'luck.' You will never hear a person talk about how unfair it is that they were able to secure an amazing job with a huge salary entirely because of their family and connections. They see this as something they have somehow earned or accomplished, or maybe credit luck if they are feeling especially humble that day.

Most people have or will lose a job or promotion to a less qualified person. Couples who cannot have children watch the purest scum of the earth procreate with rodent-like ferocity. There are around a million other examples of how brutally unfair the world can be. Because failure is no longer a motivator or remotely positive aspect of human existence, there are droves of people who are ill equipped to cope with the arbitrary unfairness of life.

Children of the Self-Esteem Movement grow into adults that cannot effectively integrate the experience of failure into their existence. They believe they are special, and believe they will succeed with regularity, because they believe that the world is a fair place. Fair, of course, meaning that things will pretty much always work out in their favor. So when (not if) these people fail as young adults (whether it was 'fair' or not) they are more likely to shut down and refuse to make another attempt. Their values have been challenged and they will not stand for it. They ignore facts in favor of concerning themselves with the perceived fairness of the situation.

Humans are not entitled to higher meaning just because we managed to develop a more efficient brain than the other animals. We are not entitled to success just because we feel special. There are not unseen forces within the universe that intervene in only human life to ensure fairness and balance. Life remains a blank and meaningless canvas for each of us no matter how much or how little self-esteem we have. Nobody is going to paint those happy little trees for you.

THE HOMICIDAL ID

Sigmund Freud was an Austrian neurologist and credited with conceptualizing and developing the field of psychotherapy in the early twentieth century. Despite having many revolutionary ideas, he is generally known for only a smattering of his stranger concepts. Introductory psychology courses rarely mention him beyond the obligation of teaching that he devised psychotherapy, had stages of psychosexual development, and is largely discredited in modern psychology.

Because of our dismissive attitude toward Freud, the extent that most people are aware of his theory is that failure to develop properly can leave a person with an anal or oral fixation. Insert requisite immature chuckling as needed. People may also be familiar with the Oedipus and Electra Complexes, but likely lack more than a cursory knowledge of them, choosing to focus only on the incestuous origins of the idea.

Freud first mentioned the concepts of the Id, Ego, and Superego in his 1923 work, appropriately titled *The Id and the Ego*. However, all of these concepts had been a subject of interest for Freud, which he discussed under different names for quite some time prior to this publication. They represent the three components of the human psyche. Freud theorized that each of them serve a specific purpose and develop at differing points during childhood. He also felt that they can develop to varying amounts based on circumstances and environment.

The Id is the only element of consciousness present at birth. It operates purely on instinct and is both incredibly primitive and impulsive. Freud thought that the Id had a particular focus on sexual and aggressive drives, and attempts to seek out immediate gratification for any impulse it has without regard to consequences. He wrote "we call it a chaos, a cauldron full of seething excitations," and that "contrary impulses exist side by side without canceling each other out."

The description of Id as chaos is appropriate. It seeks to satisfy itself by any means necessary. There is no compromise, no delay, and no failure. There is only impulse. Reward and gratification are certainties. At the risk of spoon-feeding, this sounds very much like the children of the Self-Esteem Movement.

Your Id wants to kill you. This conclusion came to me while standing on a balcony in the building where I worked. On my breaks, I would often pass the time by standing at the railing and watching the people on the lower floors go about their business. Like many other people, when I look down from a substantial height, I feel a particular sensation in my stomach, not unlike falling. This is your Id doing its best to compel you to jump, to satisfy its need for destruction. I honestly believe that this is why people are afraid of heights, not because they might fall, but because they might jump.

When it isn't trying to convince you to jump to your death, your Id wants to maim and/or destroy you in a variety of other ways. It wants you to kill people. Steal. Take drugs frequently. Fight everyone. Drive into oncoming traffic. Take food if you are hungry. Eat the people you took the food from. Cheat on your partner. Lie to your boss. Burn your house down. Rape. Pillage. Plunder. It wants you to masturbate. All the time. It's an unyielding force of nature containing nothing but the purest violence and darkest impulses of humanity. Your Id is a Viking on a healthy dose of psilocybin tea, berserking through your unconscious mind.

The Ego develops as a natural response to the Id, and serves as a force to help the Id meet its needs without causing painful consequences in the process. It helps us delay gratification in an effort to function effectively in human society. It's the primary reason that we aren't all rapists, murderers, and cannibals. However, the Ego is not without fault and impulse of its own. It deploys our defense mechanisms, potentially in an effort to justify actions taken to satisfy the Id. We use our Ego to bend our perception of reality in many ways in an effort to feel less awful about the horrible things we do when we can't keep our Id under control.

Freud believed that one's conscious awareness is contained within the Ego, making it the part of personality shaped by our experiences. We have some degree of control over the development (or lack thereof) of our Ego based on the choices we make and the experiences we engage in. We can make choices that strengthen our Ego and make it easier to quell the impulses of the Id, or we can neglect Ego development and end up with an Ego that is not strong enough to hold the Id at bay.

Because the Ego develops during childhood, it is reasonable to assume that children are not capable of handling this independently. The responsibility lies with parents and caregivers to guide children in a direction that will help them make positive choices and internalize values that will be consistent with the development of a strong and healthy Ego. The values of the Self-Esteem Movement continue to guide our culture in a direction that does not foster a strong Ego.

Finally, we develop the Superego, which is quite literally our conscience. It rewards good behavior with feelings of pride and satisfaction, and punishes bad behavior with feelings of guilt or shame. It directly impacts our Ego, which has the unfortunate task of keeping both the unyielding forces of Id and Superego in balance. The Superego represents our internalization of cultural norms and societal rules. Freud believed that this was most often learned from parental figures and caretakers during childhood.

Adults and caretakers at present are capable of remembering a time when the norms and values of our society were much more in line with producing people without the levels of instability and entitlement that currently exist. I know this because of how frequently other adults bitch about the Millennials (which usually includes Generation Y) in print and on the news. The children who currently find themselves being imparted with the values of their culture have no idea how much those norms have changed in the past twenty years. We cannot rightfully blame them for following the blueprints they were given.

None of us would hold a child accountable who thought the sky was red if that's what their parents had taught them. We would work with them, correct the problem, and probably spend a good deal of time talking badly about the parents. Without proper guidance from adults (who are aware of past values), children have no course of action but to conform to societal norms as they are presented. It is the responsibility of the adults and caretakers to hold themselves and their children to a higher standard if they truly want society to return to a less entitled state.

In a later work, Freud mentions the concept of a cultural Superego. He believed that the development of the individual mimicked the development of the culture, much in the same way that children develop in relation to their parents. If the culture has norms that are somewhat lenient regarding drug use, the individual members of that society will likely share those norms. If a society begins to uphold self-esteem, entitlement, and instant gratification, so will the members of that society.

To bring about change on an individual level, a few individuals must bring about change on a cultural level. This is where we currently find ourselves as a society. We have perverted our norms in such a way that we have negatively altered human development. The

Superego is no longer able to do its job effectively on a cultural or individual level.

Think about *The Walking Dead*, or any other zombie and/or apocalypse movie, television series, or book. A key component to telling these stories is that they take place in an environment in which the cultural Superego has been compromised or destroyed. The culture of the (usually zombie) apocalypse is one operating on Id alone.

An archetypal character that appears in all of these tales is the ruthless survive-at-all-costs person; the person who advocates stealing from other factions, preemptively killing groups of people in the name of safety, and generally revels in the lawlessness of the situation. Depending on the story, they can get somewhat rapey as well. They are the apex predators of the apocalypse because they immediately and completely succumb to the Id and rely on it to survive.

All apocalypse stories tend to have a Darwinian, survival of the fittest vibe. Fittest, in this instance is less about strong and smart, and more about ability to compromise former values and become as cruel as necessary in order to survive. Because we like to think that good and decent people will always prevail, these Id driven characters are usually killed by the hero and/or have a miraculous change of heart and die saving their group in a selfless act of redemption midway through the narrative. This portrayal is indicative of our cultural Superego – our value set suggests that morally sound people will prevail, so we tend to ignore the contrary evidence and tell stories that resonate with our preexist-ing notions. Having never been in an apocalypse, zombie or otherwise, I cannot be certain, but can pretty safely assume that the more plausible scenario involves these ruthless individuals becoming the warlord kings of the apocalypse, killing, eating, and/or enslaving those who kept control over their Id and attempted to maintain any shred of their former values.

One glorious and exaggerated example of this is Danny McBride's portrayal of himself in *This is the End.* He enters the story the morning after the Biblical apoca-lypse begins, and is channeling his *Eastbound and Down* character, Kenny Powers. After being voted out of the house for becoming increasingly driven by his Id, he ventures out into the wasteland where we assume he will die a horrible death in short order.

McBride reappears at the end of the movie as the leader of a group of cannibals with a human skull for a helm and Channing Tatum on a leash to be used for his more carnal impulses. In a matter of a few days, he goes from a slightly selfish person attempting to survive the apocalypse to a full on maniac, gorging himself on hu-man flesh and mayhem.

McBride cast his Ego and Superego aside and basked in the vicious glory of Id. It is his Id that allows him to murder people, eat them, sodomize movie stars, and gleefully pillage in any way he can imagine, all without the pesky feelings of guilt or remorse that the Ego or Superego may inflict upon him. This transfor-mation happened in a matter of days. If we were truly capable of shutting off our Ego and Superego, the change would likely happen just as quickly.

Freud believed that the Id was present at birth and represented the entirety of consciousness at that point. Over time, the Id recedes to make room for the Ego. As a child develops, the Id continues to shrink, the Ego grows, and the Superego begins to emerge. The ideal scenario involves an Id that becomes much smaller and more easily curtailed as a person ages, a Superego that isn't overly domineering, and an Ego that is strong enough to mediate the whole debacle. Society is supposed to encourage this pattern of development through rules and norms. When reality becomes distorted, the norms and values of that culture distort in response.

The norms established by the Self-Esteem Movement have created a society that is not so passively encouraging less regulation of the Id. The more powerful the Id, the less likely we are to even attempt to control our impulses. Our cultural Id is growing. The Superego is shrinking, leaving the Ego overwhelmed to the point of futility. We are becoming an increasingly impulsive and indulgent society in the aftermath of the Self-Esteem Movement.

The United States is allegedly the largest consumer of cocaine in the world. Ironically, it is also the most obese nation in the world. We have some of the highest rates of marijuana use as well, which might explain some of the obesity problem. Suicide rates are rising. Divorce rates have climbed past 50%, meaning that it is now weird to be the kid in class whose parents are still married. More than 40% of people admit to having an extramarital affair. If that weren't bad enough, approximately 70% of those people said they would have another affair if they knew they wouldn't get caught. Everybody pirates everything online. And nobody cares about any of it. We flat out refuse accountability. We are entitled to these things because we want them, and we are not in the business of waiting for, or working toward the things we think we deserve.

Your Id wants to kill you. It always has, and it always will. The Self-Esteem Movement has, and will continue to, perpetuate societal norms that encourage the Id to be larger and more powerful than the Ego and Superego, both culturally and individually. Too much of anything is never a good thing, especially when 'anything' specifically refers to the most destructive and depraved part of your unconscious mind.

An excess of Id is a horrible idea, yet we continue to encourage the growth of our cultural Id through the Self-Esteem Movement. No rational person would present a four-year-old with a Scarface-esque pile of cocaine and then put them in charge of everything. We are putting the Id, the maniacal being that lives inside of us, behind the wheel. This will not end well.

Raging Bully

It's not so much that Chris Rock is a fan of bully-ing, he just has a better way of reframing it than the rest of society. While being quasi-interviewed by Jerry Sein-feld on *Comedians in Cars Getting Coffee*, Rock said, "most kids need bullying." Of course, this was said in a hyperbolic way, but you can feel the truth behind the sarcasm. He goes on to say that the people responsible for truly amazing accomplishments were probably bullied. In a different interview, he sums up this idea by saying, "people who are bullied tend to make shit happen."

Rock understands what it means to be bullied more than most people. He was one of the first African American students to attend his elementary school. Parents and students would line the sidewalk to picket his arrival each day, calling out racial slurs, and spitting on him as he approached the building. He took this objectively negative experience, the daily misery of being bullied and discriminated against, and reframed it to become an enormous amount of motivation. I have tre-mendous admiration for those who achieve out of spite. The best revenge truly is living well.

Presently, we discuss bullying almost constantly. Boundless energy is poured into analyzing the impacts of bullying and ways in which it can be prevented. Schools, parents, and students are all hypersensitive to anything that may constitute bullying. We have become saturated with awareness. This has traditionally led people to one of two conclusions; bullying has increased significantly, or kids these days are sissies. I have typically found myself ascribing to the sissy argument, but upon further thought and investigation, I feel that a case could be made for either.

As a society, we have come to demand external validation at regular intervals to maintain an acceptable level of self-esteem. Because of this, anytime someone is unkind, or their actions do not provide validation, we often cry bully. Providing therapy to school age children frequently involves me explaining that a friend choosing not to play with you that day is not bullying. Similarly, a child not wanting to be friends, calling you a name on one occasion, or telling on you does not constitute bullying either. Parents, like their children, have become overly sensitive to negative behaviors as well. If their child is treated badly in any way, the delicate illusion of their specialness may melt away. This, as we know, is unacceptable; so parents cry foul, both loudly and often.

Fortunately, many school systems and school counselors have started incorporating strong educational components into their lessons on bullying. They are striving to define what bullying is and what it is not. The hope is that students will learn that they are not entitled to everyone being nice to them at all times and not everyone is obligated to be their friend. Negative feelings can and will happen to us all, even though none of us particularly enjoy them. Schools who embrace not education in addition to awareness are helping to undo the alarmist 'boy who cried bully' culture that has infiltrated our society.

The other side of this coin is analyzing bullying as though it has significantly increased since the nineties. Approaching this from an argument based on self-esteem presents an interesting angle. We have become horrible and narcissistic people after being consumed by self-esteem. It only makes sense that we are more likely to behave in shitty, narcissistic ways like bullying.

Once our self-esteem habit becomes too difficult to sustain on external validation alone, we must explore alternative means to get our fix. A reasonably efficient way of doing this is to reducing the self-esteem of others. Your self-esteem doesn't actually increase, but it remains higher than the esteem of those you are terrorizing. All children expect to feel special at all times; some of them will maintain these feelings by any means necessary.

The reality of the situation is that bullying is not on the rise. Contrary to popular belief, research suggests that it is actually decreasing. At least, that's what the United States government believes. Increased awareness, preventative measures, and media coverage are cited as the primary reason that people assume bullying has been steadily increasing. On their website, the coalition in charge of our national stance on all things bullying points out that the term is "often misused and misrepresented." They define bullying as a repeated pattern of negative or aggressive behavior taking place between people less than eighteen-years of age. Once again for emphasis, a repeated pattern of behavior among children. This will come up again, shortly.

The primary risk factor associated with being bullied, according to the feds, is being different than your peers. Special and unique snowflakes, indeed. We stress the value of being unique to our children to the point that it is assumed a universally positive thing, yet data show that being unique is actually the primary risk factor. Children are encouraged to be unique by parents and caregivers, while simultaneously observing the negative consequences that are sometimes associated with being different at school or in their neighborhood. The confusion caused by balancing these two realities can, and does, generate anxious kids.

An anti-bullying website (which one is irrelevant, since they all report similar statistics) found that one in seven school-aged children is a bully or victim at any given time. Fourteen percent really isn't as alarming as they want it to sound. The more concerning statistic is that 90% of children in grades 4-8 report having been bullied. That's an insane number, and cannot be indicative of the truth. What it does reflect is a society that can no longer cope with many of the negative aspects that accompany socializing with other humans. We can no longer accept that being disliked by others is not only a possibility, but a certainty. We must be included, and if we are not, then other people are being bullies. It all screams insecurity.

Supporters of both self-esteem and anti-bullying have started to combine the two issues into one very odd argument. They caution using the term bully so freely, as it may decrease the self-esteem of those labeled as bullies. I'm not exactly sure how that is supposed to work out. We are supposed to prevent bullying, but in the event that it does occur, we are to preserve the bully's positive feelings of self-worth. I'm sure that will work out just fine.

The opponents of the anti-bullying movement, which makes them the anti-anti-bullying movement I suppose, think that we have gone much too far with all of this bullying stuff. Much like the Self-Esteem Movement, the anti-bully movement encourages the externalization of negative events. If you are sad and cannot succeed, it must be someone else's fault, so we find 'bullies' to blame. This small group of folks shrewdly point out that encouraging this type of thinking in childhood has created a culture in which we frequently hear of complaints of bullying in the adult world.

Bullying in adult settings was unheard of until the snowflakes came of age. Now we regularly hear about the rampant bullying that occurs in every corner of society. It happens in offices, neighborhoods, charitable organizations, gyms, church, professional sports, universities, children's sporting events, and anywhere else occupied by more than one adult. By modern standards, I have bullied at least a few people with the content of this book.

54 million Americans feel that they have been bullied at work. There are multitudes of articles to help people deal with bullies in the workplace. Many of these

focus on what to do if your boss is a bully. In fact, 'bully bosses' comprise 72% of workplace bullies. I cannot deny the fact that these articles bring up some valid complaints such as stealing credit for their workers ideas, frequently disrespecting them, and publicly discounting their opinions. This would be upsetting to anyone, but I would be more likely to call those people assholes instead of bullies. I wouldn't feel threatened or otherwise unsafe because of it. My boss being a prick would change how I feel about my boss, not myself.

Laughably, bosses can also be considered a bully if they point out your mistakes or yell at you. As the boss, a large part of your job is to literally identify, point out, and correct mistakes. Otherwise, that employee may continue to make the same mistakes. This should not be considered bullying no matter how you twist the definition. I suppose that pointing out mistakes may devalue an employee's feelings of specialness, which is apparently more important than their actual job performance.

In my opinion, sometimes people need to be yelled at. If an employee has seriously botched something, but it doesn't warrant firing, then some good old fashioned screaming might be exactly what's needed. Bosses have yelled at me. I have yelled at my staff. It's not the nicest thing to do, but it has a time and a place. Yelling at children has become unacceptable, since it's detrimental to self-esteem. Upon reaching adulthood and entering the workforce, they are too fragile to handle a little bit of yelling. I find myself wondering if soldiers even get screamed at during boot camp anymore.

Now we are even hearing about financial bullies. I first became aware of this new phenomenon after a local news broadcast picked up the story from one of the national networks. Essentially, if your significant other is denying you access to money, credit cards, or limiting your spending, then they are a fucking bully. There was precisely zero mention of fiscal responsibility in the story. Even if you have a colossal shopping problem, or gamble away the bill money, and your partner is saving your family from financial ruin by taking the reins, they are bullying you. Externalize, externalize, externalize.

We are on a frantic Snipe hunt (look it up) to find something, anything to blame for the lack of success and happiness in our children and ourselves. Bullying happens to be an extremely convenient scapegoat for this because it already existed, was already a problem, and usually taken seriously. We have internalized the values of the Self-Esteem Movement so deeply that we cannot and will not abide negativity of our own doing. People are supposed to feel sublimely valuable and unique at all times, and there is no room for being disliked in this equation, even for legitimate reasons.

The idea that everyone should be nice at all times, and everyone should be friends sounds great on paper. Encouraging this value in school aged children was probably supposed to increase self-esteem and somehow bring about world peace. Teaching this to children gives them the false assumption that this is what adulthood will be like, hence the increasing lamentations about adult bullying.

People will not always like you, and sometimes without reason. Being a stable adult means having the ability to accept this and still feel okay about yourself. This is starkly opposed to the way we are socializing children. After contracting high self-esteem, we need everyone to like us, adore us, and be nice to us. Without constant reinforcement of our likeability, we are unable to justify the level of self-worth we are expected to have. To achieve this constant stream of reassurance we go about amassing as many friends as possible.

Again, we meditate on the wisdom of Chris Rock. Regarding bullying and school violence he said, "I didn't have six friends then. I don't have six friends now." Because he is not invested in the values of the Self-Esteem Movement, he doesn't need a collection of friends to maintain a positive self-concept. He has a family, a career, accomplishments, and reality that can all help him to validate his (probably) very realistic level of self-worth.

Perpetuating the idea that everyone should be nice and everyone will be your friend creates some very real angst in children. Many kids become distressed when there is a singular person that has no interest in being friends with them. This person may not even be particularly abrasive, just indifferent. Because some children have embraced this idea so completely, they cannot view this as an acceptable outcome.

Some children will let peers horribly mistreat them in the name of friendship. I spend a small but measurable portion of my time working with children on the idea that if a 'friend' is consistently mean to you, perhaps they aren't your friend, and devoting your time and energy into other friendships might be a more worthwhile endeavor. This makes sense to some kids, but others have difficulty understanding that friendship is a mutually positive relationship that you share with some people of your choosing. If we tracked these kids through adolescence and into adulthood, I am certain that many of them would be taken advantage of at work, mistreated by peers, and/or have a pattern of horrible relationships.

Teaching bullying in the way we currently do perpetuates the externalization and entitlement that is prevalent in the Self-Esteem Movement. We cannot be held responsible for our negative feelings – someone must have bullied us. People are supposed to be my friend and be nice to me at all times. It's not my fault that I neglected my responsibilities, I'm a victim. I don't have a spending problem, you are a financial bully.

A therapeutic technique that I (and most other therapists) seldom call upon involves reflecting the client's story back to them in such a way that they begin to feel like their own perception of events is absurd. In theory, this encourages clients to reconsider their point of view and approach their current challenge from an angle that increases their chance for overcoming that obstacle. This works particularly well for people who enjoy being a martyr. Continuously reflecting the powerlessness conveyed in their story, and pointing out each person and factor that allegedly has power over them usually takes quite a bit of wind out of their sails and gets them looking for solutions.

In the spirit of cynicism and psychoanalysis, let's take a look at my own life using the modern perception of bullying. My parents were incorrigible bullies for yelling and punishing me, even when I was wrong. My teachers were bullies for giving me poor grades when I earned them. I am bullied by the federal and state government because taxes are withheld from my paycheck. Every boss I have ever had is a bully for holding me accountable for doing my job well, and reprimanding me when I was not doing so.

My friends are bullies because they won't drop everything to hang out with me on the occasions that I have free time. For a time, my daughter was a bully because she was attached to her mother and greatly preferred her company to mine. My mortgage company bullies me because the house payment prevents my wife from being a stay at home mom, and my inability to provide this decreases my self-esteem. My wife is a terrible financial bully for making a reasonable and effective household budget that does not allow for unlimited spending on guitars and amps.

Your Id is a bully for encouraging you to act out every self-destructive impulse you have. Your Superego is a bully for trying to prevent you from engaging in the same self-destructive behaviors. Your Ego might not be a bully, but is definitely being bullied by the other two. Astoundingly, all of this bullying hasn't reduced me to a whimpering husk, unable leave my bed each morning.

Bullying is not increasing, but our awareness and (hyper) sensitivity to it has risen exponentially. The norms reinforced by the Self-Esteem Movement have blinded us. Negative feelings and negative behaviors are no longer congruent with our reality. We can't risk assuming responsibility for this, as it may jeopardize our perilously leaning tower of specialness. Externalize and avoid. Find a scapegoat and save yourself. Bullying isn't the problem, we are.

LOWERED EXPECTATIONS

I have never beaten *Super Mario Brothers.* This holds true for most of my favorite childhood video games. All of those warm and fuzzy memories of sitting in the floor of my living room, endlessly tapping away at a controller, are rife with frustration. I never finished many of these games, and didn't even come close in some cases, but I continue to cherish these memories. A sense of accomplishment came with progress. It was exciting to beat a level that had previously resulted in countless game over screens.

Games have become easier. Beating a game is an expectation in most instances, not an accomplishment or challenge. I haven't played a *Super Mario* game in years, but I imagine they are infinitely easier than their original counterparts. The same is almost certainly true for *Sonic the Hedgehog* games, if they still exist. In the *Lego Batman* games, you can't actually lose as far as I can tell, and if you appear to be stuck, Alfred almost immediately tells you what to do next. Challenge is no longer a desirable feature in video games. In fact, games that present a significant challenge, like the *Dark Souls* series, use their more traditional level of difficulty as a marketing tool.

I don't necessarily mind this, since I want to spend my limited gaming time enjoying the experience instead of being frustrated. However, this decreasing difficulty isn't confined to video games, and is indicative of how our cultural values and expectations have changed. Significantly increased self-esteem takes significantly increased reinforcement. Being unable to accomplish something difficult is detrimental to this type of inflated confidence. The reason children were able to enjoy the experience of failing countless times in the dawn of gaming is that their self-esteem accurately reflected their feelings of self-worth. Back then, we didn't need to conquer a handful of pixels to feel good about ourselves.

Today's children, with their grossly exaggerated self-esteem view difficulty and failure as contradictory to their worldview. They have been told that success is a guarantee. Special, extremely intelligent beings cannot be bested by a game. That would be absurd. Over time, games slowly became easier and easier. The racing game *Forza* has a rewind function. You can't die in the *Lego* games. There are no more game over screens.

Like video games, the rest of society has started expecting less and less of people as well. The Self-Esteem Movement created a cultural norm in which we treat people like they are extremely unique, special, intelligent, and capable of succeeding at anything just by wanting it. To keep this idea from imploding, we began expecting less of these people. Getting an A became easier. Passing your grade became easier. There were fewer rules, so staying out of trouble was easier. Impressing your parents became easier because they were told to be impressed by *anything* positive you do. Making this problem more complex, society was expecting less of children while maintaining that it has even higher expectations than before. This reinforces the factors that generate adults who are woefully confident and equally ill informed.

I have witnessed a mother fiercely argue with teachers in a school meeting that her son (who has no learning disabilities) increasing his overall average from a 25 to a 50 represented a significant improvement that should be recognized by his teachers and/or school administration. I shit you not, that actually happened, and I am still astounded that I didn't die of an aneurysm in that instant.

Parents have been encouraged to treat trying and succeeding as the same thing. Obviously, both are positive things, and should be praised, but in different ways. If a child receives the same level of praise for trying, then there is no motivation to work hard enough to succeed. Cursory effort is all that is required to obtain validation, so that's all that will be given. The other problem with lowering the bar in this fashion is that it allows for not trying to be treated as though an attempt had been made. If we praise success and attempts in the same way, then no attempt at all is more likely to elicit a 'good try' than criticism.

The purpose of adolescence is to build skills that will be vital in successfully transitioning into adulthood. The indoctrinated parents of the Self-Esteem Movement have grossly neglected this aspect of their children's development. Parenting has shifted away from skill building and focused on self-esteem and feelings of happiness. This hugely factors into the diminished work ethic of young adults currently entering the workforce.

Many developmental psychologists have been pushing for adolescence to extend into the mid-twenties after observing increasing numbers of people having difficulty transitioning into early adulthood. They are not capable of supporting themselves financially or emotionally, so stagnate in adolescence. Development grinding to a halt at this stage contributes heavily to the staggering number of college graduates that are moving home and living with their parents, often going long periods without employment.

It seems right and just to rail against these young adults. We want to shake them and scream at them until they accept their fate as an adult who must behave like one. Unfortunately, our cultural climate has slowed adolescent development to the point that people actually might not be ready for independence in their early twenties.

We are too quick to blame the economy for this trend of young adults returning to the nest that they so recently vacated. It plays a role, and certainly makes obtaining employment more difficult, especially if you insist on finding employment that pays a living wage. However, our current value system has created a culture that is decidedly opposed to overcoming a difficult job market and economy.

When the going gets tough, the snowflakes get mad and quit. We don't *do* failure, or difficulty. If we do manage to muster the perseverance to finish and fail, we can and will lament at length about the fundamental unfairness of the circumstances. For the entirety of our childhood, society has held us to such a low standard that we snap under any degree of pressure. Finding a job that is worthy of our effort may even be too much to cope with. It's much easier to retreat to your familial homestead and bitch about the economy than it is to find employment and claw your way to the position you actually want.

Because society has held my generation to a lower standard, we have started to expect less of ourselves. We are a generation of overly confident people who refuse to attempt anything that could result in frustration or failure. Without conducting a survey, I can only name a handful of people who can change the oil in their car. Or change a tire. I'm sure that I know at least a few people who don't know how to check their oil, let alone their transmission or break fluid. Accurately interpreting any of the information they glean from this is out of the question. We simply don't care. That's why there are mechanics. It's also why mechanics can charge more per hour than I can despite having gone to college for seven years and obtaining two degrees.

Similarly, we have little interest in learning about repairing things in our homes. Dishwasher breaks? Call the manufacturer. Ceiling fan needs to be replaced? Call

191

an electrician. Stove breaks? Get takeout for dinner.

The sense of pride that accompanies learning how to properly repair and maintain things is far outweighed by feelings of frustration. It's not so much that people cannot repair things, which is completely fine; it's the lack of willingness to even try or the desire to learn. There is much gratification to be had by making simple repairs in and around your household, but fear of failure and the resulting detrimental impact to self-esteem prevent many people from making an effort.

The Self-Esteem Movement created a generation of people that will do almost anything to avoid frustration. If I'm frustrated, then I'm probably not succeeding. Failure means I might not be special, which means that *my* truth might not be true at all. So instead of having a crisis of identity while trying to figure out why your washing machine is leaking all over your floor (check the drain filter), call the repair man and maintain the delicate illusion of your extreme specialty and uniqueness before your entire self-concept comes crashing down around you. Repairs are another way in which we have monetized self-esteem. It's not so much that we are buying self-esteem in this instance, but paying to keep it, membership dues to the country club of Self-Esteem.

Holding ourselves to a lower standard, while pretending that we are living up to the highest standards creates another problem. We expect less of everything. This is especially true of our consumer products. The values perpetuated by the Self-Esteem Movement have helped to create the disposable society in which we live.

People repair their homes, their cars, and some major appliances. Beyond that, everything else is disposable.

I cannot recall the last time I even heard about a television repairman. Trades like this are dying because we have little interest in repairing things when they can be replaced with something bigger, better, and newer. Compounding this issue, manufacturers are making products with components that are no longer worth repairing. Even if we wanted to repair our electronics and appliances, we usually can't. Things just break now.

Cell phones actually used to function well for more than two years. Until the advent of the smart phone, I had never replaced a phone out of necessity, or found myself counting down the days until my contract expired and I could upgrade to a properly working phone again. Now we all marvel if a phone functions well for three years. Somehow we are all completely okay with this, which is not okay.

Everything seems to break so quickly it's hard not to wonder if failure is being engineered into products to ensure ongoing sales. Loosely constructed conspiracy thinking aside, a person assembling products that will almost certainly break in a few years probably doesn't care if their workmanship adds or subtracts months or years from that product's life. I don't blame them, I would hate my job too if I knew that everything I made would be in a landfill in a couple of years.

I once watched a documentary about the Ferrari factory, during which they interviewed a number of different employees. The master mechanics who build the engines in surgically clean rooms took pride in their work. A career building some of the finest production engines in the world is something that should generate feelings of pride, especially since, aside from test driver, these are the most coveted positions in the factory. Several of the little Italian women who hand stitched the leatherwork for each interior were interviewed as well. This is a meticulous and monotonous undertaking, and easily overlooked by the public, yet these women universally expressed the same sort of pride in their work. They get excited when they see a Ferrari outside of the factory and proudly point out the stitching that might be their own.

Every person interviewed was proud to say that they manufactured Ferraris. Each day, they arrive to work in one of the most beautiful, un-factory like factories in the world. They are well compensated for the high quality of work they are expected to uphold. The most important factor, however, is they know that their work will exist and be cherished for decades. Their pride comes from the caliber of product they are making, not the working conditions or compensation. The same can't be said for the people assembling your lawnmower.

The Walton family did not necessarily invent the concept of the super store, but I still like to blame them for it. Decreasing expectations of the products we buy has helped to perpetuate the business model that allows the super stores to be such a powerful economic force. They sell goods at prices so low that it was no longer worth paying to repair them. Once that became the norm, they could begin negotiating price with manufacturers. In order to meet price points, companies must increase speed of production or decrease component quality, resulting in products that break with increasing regularity.

We are so accustomed to shoddy craftsmanship that we just expect things to break. When this inevitably happens, we drive down to the nearest super center to replace it with a newer version that is probably of slightly lower quality and will break at least as quickly as its predecessor. We are okay with this because we expect less of ourselves, and we realistically cannot hold our products to a higher standard than ourselves.

Many car manufacturers are offering warranties that would have been unheard of prior to the Self-Esteem Movement. The intended message is that they manufacture cars and trucks that are built to such high standards they are guaranteed not to break for 5 years/100,000 miles. The reality seems to be that cars are breaking with such regularity that extended warranties are a necessity to keep customers satisfied.

When my new vehicle refused to run properly due to a throttle sensor malfunction, I was livid. My old vehicles, all of the same make, some even the same model, never seemed to need anything outside of regular maintenance, yet the first time I bought something even approaching newness, it broke almost immediately. Quickly after that, it occurred to me that the factory warranty would cover the cost of the repair, and my towing service membership would deliver the vehicle to the dealer at no cost.

Once this had become clear, I was totally fine with my truck being a two-ton piece of shit sitting in my driveway. I didn't care that it was broken, because it wasn't going to cost me anything but time. I allowed the lowered standards of our culture to color my opinions about my current situation, which as a 'car guy' is a pretty embarrassing realization. The automotive industry is held to a lower standard, while pretending they hold themselves to the highest of standards by offering lengthy warranties that provide the illusion of quality.

We expect less of ourselves, so manufacturers are free to expect less of us. We expect less of our products, so manufactures have no obligation to produce goods of high quality. Car manufacturers can offer lower quality products, but keep us complacent by fixing the multitude of things that break in the first few years.

If my generation was held to a higher standard, or chose to hold ourselves to a higher standard, this would be unacceptable. Instead, we have chosen to lower expectations across the board in an effort to maintain the illusion of success. If the bar is set low enough, anyone can jump over it. I suppose the hope is that once our self-esteem finally breaks, we can pick up some newer, cheaper self-esteem at the nearest super store.

WELCOME TO THE JUNGLE

For decades now, self-esteem has been peddled to children and families like the tonics of the Old West. It was the cure, no matter the problem. Quasi-mystical properties and all sorts of flashy promises distracted potential customers from the reality that it's just some shit in a jar, probably with a lot of opium in it, ensuring that even if you weren't miraculously cured of your ailments, you at least got really, *really* high instead.

The metaphor of tonic is appropriate when discussing the Self-Esteem Movement. We all believed because we wanted to believe. It was too good to be true, too simple. But what if it *was* true? What if it really was that easy? It was too good to pass up, so we collectively gave in to the warm, syrupy high instead of finding an alternative solution.

Much like the tonics of yore, it's entirely too easy to manipulate people using self-esteem. This shouldn't be shocking since it's something that has happened for literally ever. However, it appears to be getting remarkably easier because of the incessant need for external validation that has become the norm in the wake of the Self-Esteem Movement. We have become a culture that needs to believe that we are special, and in lieu of any real evidence to support this, we look outside of our-selves to at least be *told* that we are special.

Everyone has heard a story or watched a movie with a subplot involving some bright eyed singer being taken advantage of. Maybe they sell all of their songs for a couple hundred bucks to some scumbag producer, or find themselves locked into a contract performing four-teen shows a week and paying their manager 90% of their earnings. No matter the particulars of the story, the essence is always the same, they had dreams of 'making it' and some unscrupulous person in the music industry took advantage of it by distracting them with validation. Preying upon self-esteem is not limited to the music industry. We can readily find examples of this in many other industries, most of which involve the possibility of fame and/or fortune.

Self-esteem is used in subtly predatory ways with athletes of various levels. Consider the high school star that is courted by scouts, being told he is the better than his peers. He is given his pick of universities, where he will live and be educated without expense. Attendance is optional as long as he performs on game day. Glimmers of fame begin to emerge. Thousands of people know him on campus. Perhaps his games are televised, fostering the growth of his developing celebrity. He receives special treatment because of his athletic prowess. Depending on how ethically gray the university and boosters are, he may be enjoying any number of ancillary benefits as well.

If this athlete draws the attention of professional scouts, Pandora's Box opens further still. They are quickly seduced with the possibility of making untold sums of money. Being famous *everywhere* instead of their celebrity being confined to campus. They are better than their collegiate peers. They have what it takes. Sign the dotted line. Drop out. Go pro. Fuck school, you can always go back.

This works out for many of the people presented with this situation, even though my spitefulness with regard to the amount of money professional athletes make impairs my ability to be happy for them. For some, however, the outcomes are not as much of a fairy-tale. They may experience an early career ending injury, or may not be up to the task of competing on a professional level. The result is a career cut short, far too short to have generated the earnings required to support the lifestyle they were promised. The fame and fortune to which they are entitled are no longer within their grasp.

Life quickly becomes more difficult than it ever had been before. Reenrolling in school may not be as easy as it sounded. Attendance and grades are now directly tied to your ability to show up and master the material. People treat you like another regular asshole. You are no longer special and you will not stand for it. Your only meal ticket has been punched and you are potentially left with no applicable job skills whatsoever. The ride up was amazing, but the crash after the engines of self-esteem burned out was equally devastating.

Actors and actresses, usually of the child variety, are manipulated by self-esteem in much the same way. From the time they are young, they are famous and special. They are treated much differently than their peers. Once their career begins to wane, as they always do, and they are no longer 103% special, most of these adolescents lack the appropriate coping skills to process this situation. There is a sudden and catastrophic void that was ever so recently overflowing with public adoration and validation.

There are dozens of child actors and actresses, with and without musical careers, that could easily be discussed here. My first instinct is to discuss Lindsay Lohan, but she seems quick to sue, so I will instead be talking about Brittany Spears. I don't particularly care for Brittany Spears as a musician, but for whatever reason I want to like her as a person. I genuinely like that she made a comeback and exorcised her demons of self-esteem. When I see her receiving attention for something positive, I find myself reflexively thinking 'good for her.' This is all incredibly strange to me, as this is something that has only become clear to me as I am writing it.

Brittany became famous as a child. In adolescence, we all have grandiose illusions that people are talking about us every time we enter a room. They are a natural part of development, and a large reason why teenagers behave like lunatics. These weren't delusions for people who became famous in their teens. People really were talking about them when they walked into the room.

Look at what happened to Spears. She was immensely famous in her teens and early twenties. Once that constant stream of validation slowed to a trickle she had a full on breakdown. All the barefoot in a gas station bathroom, partying, head shaving, intentional up-skirt photo stuff was done in a (potentially subconscious) effort to remain relevant. In the absence of positive attention, much like a neglected child, she attempted to reclaim any sort of attention by acting out. There's allegedly no such thing as bad press.

I don't know why this happened or how she was able to reconcile everything and resume her career. Maybe she outgrew it. Perhaps she had some issues with postpartum depression that were resolved. It could have been a carefully orchestrated comeback story. Whatever it was, I'm not unhappy that it happened.

The issue isn't Brittany Spears, or Lindsay Lohan, or Macaulay Culkin, or Corey Feldman; it's the pattern of behavior that occurs in people who become famous at a young age. The values and norms of the Self-Esteem Movement are not unlike what happens to child stars, albeit on a much smaller scale. Children and adolescents experience a massive buildup of self-worth that will abruptly end at some point during early adulthood. There is reckless disregard for what happens after that point. There is no contingency plan built into the Self-Esteem Movement to teach people how to maintain a healthy self-image independently of others.

A 2014 *Rossen Report*, clearly aimed at the alarmist portion of our society, shows just how easily young adults can be manipulated by the temptation of fame and accompanying validation. A man with a van and a camera parked near a university and asked passing students if he could interview them, presumably for

201

television. He then asked them for their driver's license and cell phone, had them complete a demographic form (including their social security number), and invited them to have a seat in the van. The report indicated that an overwhelming number of students would do all of this, often without questioning any of it, and sometimes joking about kidnapping, murder, and/or identity theft while climbing into a windowless van.

It was easy to acquire this information and get these young adults into a van because of the camera. The carrot of fame was dangling just out of reach. Maybe this would be the interview that gets them discovered. Confident of their limitless value, all they require is a springboard to catapult them into fame and fortune, which might as well be this camera toting stranger and his sketchy van.

The report concluded by cautioning parents that they may want to remind their college age children about 'stranger danger.' But these aren't kids. They are adults in every corner of the world, including our own not so long ago. What's more, none of them would have gotten into that van had the guy approached them without a camera.

Potentially dangerous strangers are not the issue that needs to be discussed with people writhing in extended adolescence. Instead, parents should consider the benefit of educating their children about the perils of assuming you should be famous and abandoning all sensibility whenever someone is going to validate this idea. Rossen did a wonderful job of showing just how easily self-esteem can be used to manipulate people, even if he didn't realize it.

Lou Pearlman made a fortune taking advantage of teenage boys. Wait, let me clarify that – Pearlman is best known for managing pretty much every monstrously successful boy band in the late nineties and early two-thousands. His business model was both simple and effective: host a talent search to find people who are driven to be famous, seduce them with said fame and fortune, and while they are still star blind have them sign horrifically predatory contracts. He was able to do this about a dozen times. Pearlman was masterful in distracting his clients with fame, while remaining focused on milking them for every dollar he could.

Eventually bands started to become aware of the overwhelmingly terrible nature of their contracts. This began when the entirety of The Backstreet Boys made $300,000 during a year in which they generated tens of millions of dollars in album sales and touring revenue. Pearlman had everyone else looking left, while he went right and collected millions in royalties as the band's producer, manager, and even the sixth member of the band. Every band he managed sued him at some point, all for undisclosed but probably similar reasons.

Pearlman was not just capitalizing on our desires to be famous; he also had a number of other ventures in which he was monetizing self-esteem in other ways. Diversity is the key when investing in anything, includ-ing the gullibility of self-esteem. For several years, he operated a talent agency, which generated income by allowing anyone to become involved with the company provided they pay for a headshot session. One can only assume that the agency did nothing beyond this.

In addition, Lou ran a Ponzi scheme that made him three hundred million dollars. Individual investors and banks were convinced to invest in companies that existed only on paper. He falsified documents to make it look legitimate, but false documents did not accomplish this on their own. Pearlman was delicately validating the self-worth of those investors. He was probably bringing them a 'special opportunity' that was not available to 'just anybody.'

The discussion of Mr. Pearlman is kind enough to transition us into talking about schemes, scams, cons and other ways that self-esteem is used to swindle people out of money. Self-esteem has become one of our most important currencies. Many shrewd and unethical people are trading this currency for the sort that actually buys you things.

There seem to have been a recent resurgence of pyramid schemes, many of which are based on beverages of some kind. One that became relatively popular is Verve energy drink, distributed by a company called Vima, which apparently has a variety of triangular business models in which you can participate. This is like the majority of product based pyramid schemes – the lowly builders of the pyramid buy the products up front as 'samples' and go about harassing people to buy the rights to sell them, while the pharaohs at the top of the pyramid are busy counting their money.

I recently browsed the Facebook pages of several people who are involved in selling Verve, as well as the page for Vima itself. Shocking amounts of stupidity were smeared across each profile. One young man claims, "I'm in the 3% because I made the decision that I would be there eventually." There was nothing to indicate exactly which three percent he is including himself in, I just hope that I am not a part of it.

Probably the best quote gleaned from the depressing hilarity of browsing these pages was "I'm going to make it because I believe in myself." First of all, no you aren't. Secondly, if you believe in yourself, shoot higher than selling energy drinks for a living, even if they aren't entangled in a pyramid scheme. If the only requirement for success is believing in yourself, then everyone would be successful. Being confident in yourself and your abilities is a wonderful thing, but certainly isn't the only requirement for achievement.

Vima has successfully tapped into the cultural mindset of the Self-Esteem Movement. They teach their 'employees' that they can be successful just because they want to be. They push the idea that shilling their drinks makes you a self-employed businessman, making you better than your peers who are stupidly working at a job where they don't have to pay their employer.

Vima is capitalizing on our cultural gullibility when it comes to being told we are special. Tell us we are special and better than everyone else and we are putty in your hands. Take advantage of us all you want, just validate us. You are special and will be successful. You can and become rich and famous without even breaking a sweat! How exciting! Now pay for this crate of energy drinks and get the fuck out of my office.

I would not be surprised to see schemes of all sorts gaining momentum in our esteem driven society. Self-esteem itself is essentially a Ponzi scheme. The short-term returns on infusing children with maniacal levels of self-esteem were phenomenal. We immediately reinvested, assuming that we had found the solution to all of our cultural woes. The returns were unbelievable, even better than our initial investment. It wasn't too good to be true, no sir. We were special, and special people get lucky. Special people succeed without trying. We put everything on the line the next time, every moral and value we could find in every nook and cranny of society. Predictably, the rug was then pulled from under us, and we were left culturally destitute.

Religions, cults, and other spiritual endeavors are not spared the impact of self-esteem either. The most obvious example of this is Scientology, which if you will notice I will not be calling a cult even once. In order to progress through the ranks of the church, one must give and give generously. Those who cannot or do not give are somehow unworthy of the sacred knowledge of their faith. Money buys superiority through exclusive knowledge. It buys power and influence. It probably infuses you with more of whatever it is that Dianetics measures. Money does all of this, but mostly it pays for your spiritual self-esteem. I'd be willing to bet that the percentage of people reaching the upper echelons of Scientology have steadily increased since the Self-Esteem Movement began.

By linking money directly to the amount of knowledge you receive, Scientology capitalizes on self-esteem. As with any leveled cultural system, those on the top feel superior to those on the bottom, and those at the bottom crane their necks (and in this case, wallets) to reach the upper tiers. Say what you will of Hubbard, the man knew how to structure a successful religious business model.

Christianity itself has seen a shift in thinking. In recent years, it has focused on being more motivational and 'feel good' than ever before. I have not attended a church service in a substantial amount of time, so I have no real way of knowing how pervasive this shift has been, but there is abundant evidence of it in the way that practicing Christians convey their teachings in their everyday lives.

I cannot remember the last time I heard someone quoting the Old Testament aside from condemning homosexuality. Even televangelists have moved away from delivering sermons from the Old Testament. I find this both interesting and a bit disturbing, since hellfire and brimstone have traditionally been the bread and butter of televangelists. Be a Christian, and be a good one, or be prepared for eternal damnation. Tithes and offerings are often entangled in these heated sermons. Give and ye shall be saved.

On many Sundays, I find myself up with the dawn hanging out with my seven month old daughter. I like to have some noise in the background on these early mornings, and my taste in music isn't exactly crusty eyed predawn material for babies and sleepy fathers. Since we no longer see fit to pay for cable (yep, we are *those* people), more often than not there is a televangelist quietly delivering a sermon to my empty living room while my daughter plays or eats breakfast.

These reverends, preachers, and pastors no longer seem to be talking about the vengeful, angry God that their predecessors spoke of. Instead, they have adopted a more positive, uplifting approach. They are usually preaching from the New Testament, which isn't unusual given its much more positive outlook on, well, everything. The tone has changed from 'believe or else' to 'believe and all of your problems will disappear.'

I have heard a televangelist say with conviction that if you believe in God, He will take your problems away. If only we believe, we will be happy and carefree for the rest of our days. Jesus, take the wheel. I'm putting you in charge so I don't have to be. I have let go; now it's up to the Almighty to fix my every concern. It makes me throw up in my mouth a little just thinking about it.

This 'give it to God' mentality is nothing more than a spiritual (and arguably positive) way of externalizing your problems. Many people are quick to take credit for their accomplishments, but will immediately defer any and all difficulties to the Good Lord. I am special and made in God's own image, therefore He cares about me very specifically and will not allow me to endure any sort of hardship without intervening. I am special; Jesus will get this one for me. We have come to believe that we are entitled to happiness and comfort to such a degree that many of the more religiously inclined have come to expect divine intervention rather than actually working to solve their difficulties.

Our cultural mindset has shifted in such a fundamental way that it has changed the way that Christians choose to worship. It admittedly gets old to hear sermons about damnation and hellfire every Sunday morning. Seeing arenas disguised as churches reinforce our societal specialness and penchant for externalization is just as likely to find me rolling my eyes at how disgustingly pandering it all is.

In most of America's history, Christianity had a large influence over the development of culture. This is the first instance in which I can recall a societal movement having a significant impact on Christian culture. It's terrifying to think that such a poorly thought out idea has been able to have so much influence.

If you let go of your steering wheel and expect divine intervention, you are probably going to die in a fiery crash. Jesus does not have time to correct your awful driving or bratty expectation that he should miraculously fix all of your problems. Take some responsibility for yourself and stop being such a fucking martyr. No matter how hard you try, you simply cannot out martyr Jesus.

Self-esteem has long been used as a currency to manipulate people. We commonly observe this in the sports and entertainment industries, but can easily see glimmers of it linked to things like pyramid schemes, and spirituality. Everywhere you turn there are boundless opportunities to exploit self-esteem. Take my money. Take my pride. Do what you will, just make me feel special while you are doing it.

FROM THE SHOULDERS OF GIANTS

Discussion about self-esteem and its value is not a new topic. The merit or detriment of self-esteem in varying quantities has been debated for centuries. There have always, and will always be people on both sides of the issue. This is mostly due to the fundamental differences in which philosophers, researchers, and people in general have chosen to define and measure self-esteem.

As with many philosophical discussions, it seems prudent to start with the thoughts of someone Greek. For our purposes, let us consider Socrates. He believed that the beginning of wisdom is knowledge of oneself. We must know ourselves before we can know anything else. Kahlil Gibran reiterates this as "Knowledge of the self is the mother of all knowledge." While neither idea specifically focuses on self-esteem, both are applicable when discussing the Self-Esteem Movement.

The Self-Esteem Movement discourages children and adolescents from developing accurate knowledge of self. We are no longer supposed to know that we are bad at things, as this may lower self-esteem. Instead we have encouraged children everywhere to embrace a horribly inflated and inaccurate self-image, one in which they are superhero, supermodel, supergeniuses without flaw and beyond reproach. If one is in agreement with Socrates and/or Gibran, then the Self-Esteem Movement represents a sizeable obstacle in gaining knowledge of anything by making it difficult to ascertain accurate information about oneself.

Aristotle weighed in on the subject of self-esteem as well. He felt that self-esteem was "akin to magnanimity (greatness of soul), which is existing between vanity and cowardice. We must not be overly weak, but we must avoid arrogance."

We require feelings of self-worth to advocate for ourselves, stand up for our beliefs, take chances, or risk seeking out the love of another. Too little self-esteem prevents us from attempting this. Too much will result in arrogance and frustration when confronted with failure. The Self-Esteem Movement discourages indulging in moderation, which Aristotle would view as encouraging arrogance, anger, and aggression.

Søren Kierkegaard went to great lengths in his works on love to differentiate between appropriate and inappropriate self-love, and spoke about inappropriate self-love like a perversion. Once a person loves himself too much, it is detrimental to himself and to his relationships. Obviously, this is in direct conflict with the teachings of the Self-Esteem Movement, which maintains that a person cannot possibly love himself too much (or maybe even enough). Kierkegaard believed that an excess of self-love made one prone to egomania, which very rarely leads to favorable outcomes in life, love, or happiness.

Russian philosopher and mother of Objectivism, Ayn Rand spoke often (and at length) about self-esteem. She believed that high self-esteem was a necessity for one to achieve an adequate and satisfying quality of life. Many of her thoughts on self-esteem seem congruent with the intended values of the Self-Esteem Movement, but I imagine that she would absolutely despise the movement itself. Rand thought that esteem and love were commodities to be earned, but from her statements and actions, she seemed to believe that once a person is of high self-esteem, she may conduct herself in any way she sees fit. The Self-Esteem Movement is very much in line with this thinking, but eliminated the difficult bits about working hard and earning things.

Rand believed that it was immoral to love others more than oneself, and actually deemed it impossible to do so because "the man who does not value himself, cannot value anything or anyone." In a way, this harkens back to the teachings of Socrates – we must understand ourselves before we can venture to understand, and therefore value, anything else. Of course, where Socrates might have made a case for moderation of self-esteem, Rand seems to endorse stockpiling self-esteem.

Nathanial Branden was the protégé of Ayn Rand and helped her to establish the Objectivist movement. He wrote works focused on self-esteem including *The Psychology of Self-Esteem* and *The Six Pillars of Self-Esteem*. Since that time, Branden has continued to advocate for high self-esteem, but stresses that it must be based in rationality. He believed self-esteem is "always a positive concept" and that it is impossible to have too much of it.

Despite his enthusiasm for large amounts of self-esteem, Branden stresses that it is not a "free gift of nature" but something that has to be cultivated and earned for oneself. In order to effectively do this, we need to live with congruence, which requires choosing behaviors that are in line with our personal value set. Doing this generates feelings of integrity, which leads to increased feelings of self-esteem.

Branden felt that having "respect for reality" is a vital part of building authentic self-worth. To respect reality, we must first acknowledge it. By creating a culture in which it is increasingly difficult to accurately assess your own strengths and weaknesses as a child or adolescent, the Self-Esteem Movement discourages the acknowledgement or respect of reality.

Branden spoke about the differences between genuine and pseudo self-esteem exhaustively. Pseudo self-esteem is built upon external factors like possession, the approval of others, wealth, and achievements that are given instead of earned. These feelings of worth change rapidly and drastically because one seeking out self-esteem in this manner requires constant success or other demonstrations of validation. Genuine self-esteem, on the other hand, is generated by our internal values and the effort that allowed us to achieve, not from the act of achieving itself. Branden believes that this makes genuine self-esteem more stable and consistent because one's values do not quickly change, and respecting one's own efforts is not necessarily tied to success or failure in a particular endeavor.

Branden most concisely expressed his thoughts on self-esteem by defining it as "the experience of being competent to cope with the fundamental challenges of life and as being worthy of happiness." Having genuine self-esteem means accepting and coping with difficulties while remaining a generally happy and stable human being. Not that there will never be storms, but we will be well equipped to weather them.

Many and more followers of Rand, Branden, and Objectivist philosophy continue to express similar opinions. Self-esteem remains an unquestionably positive thing in their opinion, and the more one has, the better. However, the trend has been to very clearly explain that the self-esteem observed in many people is not genuine self-esteem. It would seem that even the fiercest champions of self-esteem feel the need to distance themselves from the Self-Esteem Movement. Some Objectivists have published articles that specifically speak out against the practices of the Self-Esteem Movement, which one might assume is exactly what Rand would be doing were she still among the living.

Because feelings of worth are so intertwined with therapy, many of the great therapists have discussed self-esteem in their theories, research, and practice. Since the act of therapy is not exactly a scientific endeavor, there are numerous divergent opinions on self-esteem, how it should be addressed, and what purpose it serves within the psyche of a human being.

I have a Warhol print of Sigmund Freud hanging in my office, but only because I was unable to find a print of Carl Rogers that was to my liking. Carl Rogers is the father of modern therapy, and developed a much more genial approach to treatment than his clinically minded forbearers had utilized. His theory is called Humanistic, Person Centered, or Rogerian, all of which pretty much mean 'friendly.' Imagine if Mr. Rogers (of neighborhood fame) came in each day, changed his shoes and cardigan, and proceeded to provide therapy for a number of different people instead of talking to puppets. That is basically how the other Mr. Rogers went about things, and it works surprisingly well.

One of Rogers' core concepts is the idea of unconditional positive regard, which means that one must view his clients in a positive light at all times. He felt that we must identify some redeeming factor in the client in order to effectively work with them. This is to prevent the client from feeling like the counselor is being judgmental of his actions, which is the second of three core concepts of Rogerian therapy. The third is genuineness, for both the client and the therapist. Therapists encourage clients to reach this state of honesty with oneself, but must also exhibit this quality in order to be taken seriously by the client. I choose to bore you with this brief lesson in counseling theory because, at first glance, Rogerian theory sounds a whole lot like the bullshit being shoveled onto us by the Self-Esteem Movement. We are all positive, should never be judged, and are all special and unique little snowflakes.

Carl never officially discussed the Self-Esteem Movement to my knowledge, but had plenty to say about self-esteem, most of which was in stark contrast to the culture and values of the Self-Esteem Movement. Rogers fundamentally agreed with Abraham Maslow's thoughts on self-esteem – once basic physiological needs are met, one can focus on higher order needs such as love, a sense of belonging, and self-esteem. Cultivating self-esteem requires an environment of "genuineness, acceptance, and empathy." Therein lies the foundation of the conflict between Rogers and the Self-Esteem Movement.

The Self-Esteem Movement in no way encourages genuineness. It teaches us to have a false concept of our abilities and ourselves. It actively discourages acceptance of things like reality, responsibility, failure, or fault. By reinforcing increased focus on self, it discourages empathy, because the victims of the Self-Esteem Movement simply do not have to time to focus on *other people.* Empathy is a dangerous proposition when your culture has determined that your primary developmental task as a child and adolescent is to be extremely selfish. Forgetting to focus on yourself and your own unique specialness might mean a blow to your self-esteem, which might make you less special than you previously thought, which is just not an option.

Rogers universally encouraged self-actualization and congruence in his clients. The concept of self-actualization is self-explanatory – you obtain a high degree of knowledge about yourself and actively work toward becoming the idealized version of yourself. The self-esteem pumped into the children of today works against this concept by clouding their ability to gain relevant knowledge about themselves. Congruence means that your ideal self matches your actual behaviors. While the Self-Esteem Movement has encouraged the development of ideal self in all people, it does so with the least effort possible. We have been encouraged to think of ourselves as ideal, but not to strive toward becoming better people. Perhaps it would be better to say that the Self-Esteem Movement encourages the development of the idol self, which we dutifully worship at the altar of our greatest of deities, Self-Esteem.

Self-esteem forms in childhood by interacting with parents, according to Rogers. False interactions result in false self-esteem. What he infers is that parents must be genuine and empathetic so their children can model and internalize these behaviors. However, it can be viewed within a cultural context as well. As time progresses, people who have been adversely impacted by the Self-Esteem Movement will have more and more children. These people are at increased risk of having a false self-concept, and therefore operate at a diminished capacity to convey genuineness to their children. Extrapolating this shows that this new generation begins life with a false sense of self and shaky self-esteem, then begin school only to be indoctrinated with the lingering effects of the Self-Esteem Movement. This has the potential to have a far worse impact on future generations than it has on my own simply because many of us are no longer capable of behaving genuinely.

Rogers most plainly spoke about self-esteem when discussing the differences between people of high and low self-worth. People of high self-worth are capable of accepting failure and facing challenges in life. People of low self-worth tend to avoid challenges and have difficulty accepting failure or unhappiness as part of the human experience. Rogers' thoughts on self-esteem are completely opposite the results of the Self-Esteem Movement. High self-esteem has become tenuous and full of anxiety about failure for fear that it will decrease our most precious commodity. People of lower (probably normal and healthy) self-esteem are far more likely to face a challenge and (gasp) learn something about themselves in the process, all because they are not preoccupied with maintaining the unrealistic level of externally driven self-esteem that has become the norm.

Positive self-regard is the Rogerian concept of learning to view oneself in a positive way without external reinforcement. Creating a generation of people that require consistent external validation to maintain their level of self-esteem goes against this idea entirely. If we are constantly seeking out validation, we may never learn to generate an authentic view of ourselves. In many cases, this authenticity means a decrease in perceived self-esteem, but it seems like more than a fair trade when you receive a more accurate and stable self-concept in return.

Albert Ellis is best known for developing Rational Emotive Behavioral Therapy, which was a precursor to Cognitive Behavioral Therapy, the preferred modality of many therapists of today. More importantly than any of that, Ellis *hated* self-esteem, which obviously means that he will be discussed with exuberance.

The Myth of Self-Esteem, which Ellis published in 2005, begins with the simple question, "Is self-esteem a sickness?" Ellis being the man that he was, goes about answering this question immediately, saying that self-esteem is "probably the greatest emotional disturbance known to the human race." He felt that people were overly dependent on generating and validating feelings of self-esteem, and that too much self-esteem is equally as detrimental as too little self-esteem.

Much like Branden, Ellis makes a clear distinction between unconditional self-acceptance and conditional self-esteem. As you may have guessed, unconditional self-acceptance represents internally driven feelings of self-worth, and conditional self-esteem is reliant on external factors. He felt that looking outward for validation of self-worth was an act of betrayal, saying that "tying our self-esteem to the approval of 'significant others,' and betraying our own judgment in the process, is one of the tragic mistakes by which we can betray ourselves. But it is a common one." With this, Ellis points out that we are a culture with flawed methods of self-evaluation.

Conditional self-esteem is built upon external approval and achievement. Ellis found this to be an unfair way of assessing worth since we are human, and humans are imperfect creatures that fail with regularity. This generates feelings of self-worth that are fleeting and inconsistent. We begin to operate under ever increasing stress because we are constantly seeking out the approval of others, which in many cases, requires us to continue to improve well beyond what should be necessary to generate positive feelings of self-worth. Because most people are seeking out conditional self-esteem, they tend to shy away from behaviors or risks that may result in failure. They need to succeed in order to maintain their self-esteem, and would rather do nothing than chance failure.

In his memoir, Richard Nixon admits that he felt *nothing* when he learned that he had won reelection. He was expecting a rush of positive feelings and increased self-esteem, but there was nothing. Congratulations, you have been reelected as one of the most powerful people in the world, and then nothing. This is only possible because Nixon was presumably evaluating himself in an external way, and keeping his job was not a gratifying experience. He was already doing his job. There was no more room for improvement, and therefore, no way to improve his position and obtain further validation. Even Presidents lack stable feelings of self-esteem if they cultivate worth outside of themselves.

Roy Baumeister is the most interesting person to ever study self-esteem. He first began researching self-esteem as an undergraduate psychology student at Princeton in 1973. The results of his initial studies were overwhelmingly positive – people who are experiencing any number of problems or strife in their lives also rated low on measures of self-esteem, and those raking high on self-esteem seemed to lack these problems. He continued to research self-esteem through his graduate and doctoral programs at Princeton. All of his studies continued to indicate that high self-esteem was the solution to many of the problems observed in our culture.

Concerning his research, Baumeister said, "We figured that if we could boost self-esteem, we not only could learn about ourselves but maybe do some good for society...And it was easy to get good data. So, all this made me think I was onto something good." It's incredibly easy to become enamored with good data. When the data come back in an overwhelmingly positive way, you may find yourself chasing dragons just because the numbers appear to support your hypothesis.

By the late 1980's, Baumeister was beginning to doubt his earlier conclusions as more and more research on self-esteem was being published. It seemed to him that increasing self-esteem was doing very little to solve the problems of our society, and might be creating some entirely new problems as well. He began to think that many of the positive outcomes associated with high self-esteem could just as easily be the result of things such as a stable home environment or a trusting relationship with caregivers. Baumeister continued to research self-esteem, but was more concerned with the potentially negative outcomes of extremely high self-esteem.

In 2000, Baumeister and a small group of his peers were commissioned by the American Psychological Society to conduct a meta-analysis of all research done on the subject of self-esteem. After completing the review, he and his team concluded that the benefits of self-esteem had been greatly exaggerated at best and complete fallacy at worst. They found that inflated levels of self-esteem in adolescents were associated with slightly higher levels of alcohol consumption, sexual promiscuity, drug taking, and little else.

Children with high self-esteem do not get better grades, although they were able to determine that achieving something positive usually increases a child's of self-esteem. High self-esteem does not increase work performance, but it does increase a person's rating of their performance. Having high self-esteem helps you feel better about yourself, not actually *be* better.

Much to my delight, Baumeister even went as far as to speak specifically about the self-esteem task force and their movement. He said, "the task force members – like many of us – were undeterred by the weakness and ambiguity of the evidence suggesting a benefit in boosting self-esteem; we all believe the data would come along in good time." The initial findings were good, and it seemed like a good (and relatively easy) idea to implement, so everyone blindly hoped it would work. Many initiatives and movements begin this way, and there is usually nothing wrong with that. The difference is that the Self-Esteem Movement dug in and refused to give up. Like a product of itself, it refused to acknowledge failure or a lack of specialness.

With regard to criminality and/or violence, Baumeister points out that many violent people or groups often rate very highly on self-esteem measures. He thought that this might actually perpetuate some of the violence seen in this population. When not shown the respect that they 'deserve' many people of this ilk respond violently. They feel entitled to the immediate respect of anyone they encounter because they think very highly of themselves. They shouldn't have to *earn* anything. This entitlement may factor into their criminal undertakings as well, but that's another matter entirely.

I have observed this in my own work with inmates and gang members. Respect is the order of the day and is just as important as money to many of these young criminals. I have been regaled with many tales of shoot-ings, stabbings, fights, and revenge based entirely on a perceived act of disrespect. In the majority of these instances, the person seated across from me had been swallowed up by the Self-Esteem Movement.

Respect is something they feel entitled to, and most of these young men and women assured me that a person earns their respect by showing respect first. I pose the same question to most clients in this situation – 'What happens if you come across another person who feels the same way that you do? What if that person feels like *you* must be the first one to show respect?' Nearly every answer is some variation of 'that wouldn't happen' or 'people know me and know to respect me' or 'I guess we would have a problem then.' When an unstop-pable force meets an immovable object, the results are rarely positive.

Baumeister built his career upon researching self-esteem and advocating for increased self-esteem for all people. Where he differs from many researchers and people in general, is that he was willing to reassess his opinions and research when the data stopped making sense. Once Baumeister started speaking out against self-esteem, Nathanial Branden questioned his methods and suggested that his findings were flawed due to not properly differentiating self-esteem from narcissism. I am inclined to side with Baumeister on this issue because he was willing to approach the issue in a scientific way despite the risk of invalidating a large portion of his own research. The data no longer supported his initial findings, and he was unwilling to change the way he defined things to make it do so.

Having spent decades consistently researching self-esteem, Baumeister concluded that we should stop placing such high value on self-esteem, and begin to focus on developing self-control. He felt that an appropriate level of self-control can help to alleviate many of the problems that have been traditionally blamed on low self-esteem including drug abuse, violent behavior, and poor school performance. Not only that, but instilling a person with self-control has a far greater chance of helping him to become a better person instead of simply thinking of himself as a better person. This sounds like a good idea, and it probably is, although the same thing could be said about self-esteem twenty-something years ago. The key will be to maintain moderation in whatever course we choose as a culture.

After devoting three decades to researching self-esteem, Baumeister summed up his thoughts on the matter by saying, "Despite my years invested in research on self-esteem, I reluctantly advise people to forget about it." The research failed to show long term benefits. Being a scientist, but also decent human being, he was able to acknowledge that his hypothesis was wrong and move on to other areas of research. Having avoided indoctrination by the Self-Esteem Movement, his self-esteem has remained unphased.

EVERYTHING IS AMAZING, AND NOBODY IS HAPPY

Louis Szekely, better known as Louie C.K., often draws comparisons to the late, great George Carlin. Every generation has at least one George Carlin, an entertainer who is unflinching in the face of political correctness, societal norms, and generally says the things that need to be said. Richard Pryor, Lenny Bruce, Chris Rock, Bill Hicks, Bill Burr and David Cross could all be substituted for Louie or George in this argument. What sets these comedians apart from the other great stand-ups is their ability to convey controversial observations of culture. This type of comedy makes us laugh, but sometimes encourages us to think about cultural issues that we might otherwise be too uncomfortable to consider or even acknowledge. This is why I will always regard stand-up comedy as a noble undertaking.

George Carlin even had a bit about self-esteem ruining children, in which he calls it "child worship." He points out that eliminating winners and losers decreases self-awareness. He berates the education system for reducing the requirements for honor roll to "having a body temperature somewhere in the nineties." He posed the question of exactly when special children become unspecial adults, stating that if we are all truly special, then the whole idea behind the Self-Esteem Movement loses its meaning. Basically, George Carlin summarized the majority of this book in approximately four minutes.

While it's true that every generation has someone like Carlin, this generation differs in that we *need* one. Comedians like Louie C.K. and Bill Burr are offering a much needed counterpoint to the norms we have adopted as a society. We are socialized to believe that, under no circumstances should we ever communicate in such a way that will be offensive to another person. We should consider the feelings and values of other people before we voice an opinion, an idea that is good in theory. Of course people should behave in ways that take other people into consideration. 'Do unto others' and just about a thousand other variations of the golden rule exist in cultures and religions around the world. Like most things, we have taken this idea too far, in part because of the Self-Esteem Movement, and have managed to drive this principal into absurdity.

Political correctness is a term popularized in its modern connotation in the late 1980s and early 1990s. People continue to throw this term around, usually in a pejorative sense. The basic principal is that people should not use 'politically incorrect' terms in an effort to avoid offending anyone, anywhere, at any time, for any reason. Incorrect, in this context, meaning anything offensive or even mildly controversial.

Once politically correct had worked its way into our vernacular, most comedians already had a bit about it. George Carlin did. Ralphie May named one of his specials *Just Correct* in which he has a lengthy bit about his decision to forgo efforts to be politically correct and focus on being 'just correct.' Bill Maher went as far as naming his show *Politically Incorrect*. If an idea is immediately this easy to make fun of, it was probably never a good idea.

Political correctness spiraling out of control in tandem with the Self-Esteem Movement is not coincidence. Increasing priority was placed on maintaining high self-esteem. To accomplish this, it became necessary to create a culture where anything that would potentially diminish self-esteem would be outwardly discouraged. We had the right to high self-esteem, but not necessarily the right to free speech or a differing opinion.

Over diagnosis of mental health issues in children is one way to illustrate how out of hand self-esteem and political correctness have gotten. In the nineties, every child who had behavioral issues and/or academic difficulties was diagnosed with ADHD. They were then heavily medicated with varying degrees of success (usually failure). They can't be blamed for their poor impulse control, they have a disorder.

After society collectively decided that ADHD was being recklessly over diagnosed, they moved on to Bipolar Disorder. In the early 2000s, children with difficulty controlling aggressive behaviors, especially at school, were vigorously diagnosed with Bipolar Disorder. Again, they hold no responsibility for their actions – they're afflicted. The most recent trend has been diagnosing

Asperger's Disorder when a child has poor social skills and/or a low frustration tolerance. Since it is especially distasteful to reprimand a child who has a developmental disability, a diagnosis of Asperger's Disorder further insulates the child from accountability for their actions.

Prevalence of ADHD is listed as 3%-7% in school age children. Bipolar Disorder affects approximately 1% of the general population. Data on the prevalence of Asperger's Disorder is listed as 'lacking' by the Diagnostic and Statistical Manual of Mental Disorders (DSM IV-TR). More than 7% of children were diagnosed with ADHD in the nineties. Children continue to be diagnosed with Bipolar Disorder well beyond its stated prevalence. Obviously, there are clear cases of these disorders in which the child truly does have a mental health issue, but these seem to be in the minority.

The sad reality is that many children are diagnosed with a disorder when they just have poor coping skills, or are the product of a parenting style that is some combination of lazy, indulgent, and ill informed. Parents reap the rewards of this decision by eliminating many difficult aspects of parenting. They also gain an incredibly effective way to excuse their parenting and/or their child's behaviors. They are able to preserve the specialness of their child (and sometimes themselves) without putting in the work to correct the root cause of the issue (which is usually their parenting).

It seems counterproductive to label children with disorders as a method of preserving self-esteem. Most people would assume that having a disorder would be much more likely to lower self-esteem. However, in this instance a disorder that you cannot control is preferable to making poor choices. When put into that context, the disorder provides the child (and parents) a way to ignore completely controllable aspects of personality that could decrease feelings of self-esteem. If a child cannot effec-tively cope with being told no, they might not be special. If a child lacks the social skills to adequately make friends, they might not be that special. But, if they have an uncontrollable disorder that prevents them from being able to do these things, then they are still obviously and inherently special, they just have a disorder.

A silver lining to my qualms with the number of children diagnosed with Asperger's recently arrived on my desk. The DSM-V has been published and will be put into use in 2015. Among the changes made is the exclu-sion of Asperger's Disorder, which has been collapsed into Autism Spectrum Disorder, where it should have rightfully been placed all along. Asperger's is usually described as high functioning Autism, or a disorder akin to Autism without significant intellectual impairment. This is not necessarily a negative thing, but by giving it a different name, it became much easier to for adults to label children with this disorder.

A diagnosis of Autism continues to carry a high degree of stigma in the general population. Now parents will have to decide between taking ownership of their child's inability to effectively socialize and regulate their emotions, or label them with a disorder is accompanied by sizeable negative stereotypes. I am choosing to view this as a sign that people will be less likely to seek out a disorder to label their child unless their child truly is showing signs and symptoms of a particular disorder. I will now step down from my soapbox and return my attention to the subject at hand.

Comics like Louie C.K. and Bill Burr have careers built upon our need for a counterpoint to the neutered way we are taught to socialize and express ourselves. We have become ingrained with the idea that damaging a person's self-esteem is quite nearly the worst thing we can do. Most of us will only half-heartedly express our most powerful convictions if there is even a chance of offending somebody.

Even now, I wonder if my writing will offend, or otherwise negatively impact any of the people I have mentioned by name. I hate feeling this way. I have the right to my opinions, and the right to express them. Unfortunately, exercising that right has become a Herculean challenge in our culture. This is what makes Louie C.K. and his peers so necessary and refreshing. It is a glorious thing to watch a person sell out a theater and openly state opinions that the rest of us would be ridiculed for voicing publicly. It gives the rest of us hope – if they can express themselves honestly, maybe I can too.

Bill Burr stood on stage in Philadelphia and launched into a brutal tirade, ripping out the very soul of the city for eleven minutes. In Philadelphia, a city that takes pride in their excessively violent sports fans. This was not what he went there to do. He had a set prepared and had intentions of delivering his regular act. After watching an opening comic being booed and mistreated by the crowd, Burr decided to scrap his set and reflect some of that malice back to the audience and city. All of the material was improvised, and was full of very real disdain.

The rational ending of this story is that he was booed off stage and assaulted in the parking lot as he left, never to play Philly again. Instead, the initial boos gave way to cheers and laughter as he eviscerated the city and citizens of Philadelphia. The crowd appreciated his authentic expression of emotion and opinion much more than they cared about what he thought of their city. He was later invited back to perform at the Tower Theater, one of the more iconic venues in the city. This is irrefutable proof that we have a need for honest expression and freedom of speech.

Louie C.K.'s career has thrived in response to the Self-Esteem Movement. His career really began to take off around 2007, which I have arbitrarily chosen because that was around the time I first heard people mention him who typically didn't follow stand-up comedy. Louie has been a working stand-up since the late eighties, but his style has evolved over the years. He has always been relentlessly funny, that much hasn't changed. However, his act has become more controversial and vulgar over time, which also makes it more authentic.

Louie is completely unafraid to speak his mind on stage, regardless of the issue, potential for offense, or context. As self-esteem gained momentum through the nineties, so did he. As the general population became afraid to offend anybody, he became more willing to do so. He is the much needed counterpoint to the way we are expected to express ourselves, and should be given some sort of humanitarian award for freedom of speech.

Appearing on *The Late Show* with Conan O'Brian in 2008, Louie told an anecdotal story about wifi not working on a flight and how upset some passengers became because of this. He riffed for a couple of minutes about how cell phones and wireless internet and airplanes are essentially miracles, but we don't care and are sometimes dissatisfied with them even if they are working perfectly. He summed up the whole idea with "everything is amazing, and nobody's happy."

This is true to an absolutely sickening degree. We are impulsive, impatient, demanding, entitled, and horrible people. I cannot rightfully blame the Self-Esteem Movement for all of this, but I can say with confidence that it has reinforced these qualities to the point that they now represent the societal norm. I curse at my phone when the internet doesn't load quickly enough. I go briefly insane when a streaming movie or television show lags or stops. Everyone I know does something similar.

Only a few years ago, I had never owned a phone that could check email and had no idea that I would soon be able to stream shows and movies directly to my television. As a culture we have stopped being amazed with things. We are no longer content with the magical devices we are given. We just get mad at them, and feel entitled to things that work exactly how we expect them to for every second of every day. Jaded doesn't even begin to describe it.

Louie C.K. also writes, directs, produces, edits and stars in a critically acclaimed show that airs on FX. The show, appropriately named *Louie*, incorporates bits of his standup and chronicles the life of a fictitious version of himself. Instead of filming his show through rose-colored lenses, he has chosen a bleaker, more depressing path. Louie is willing to show his character as successful, yet unhappy at times. He is unafraid to have a show that embraces the negative emotions that every human experiences with regularity.

People appreciate this level of honesty. I feel more connected to the show because it feels more like real life. Things never resolve perfectly 100% of the time, which makes it much easier to identify with a show like *Louie* than a typical 'sitcom.' *Louie* is a show that refuses to reinforce the idea that we are entitled to happiness, which is part of what makes it so great, and also what makes it difficult for some people to watch.

SECOND AXIS

Psychiatrists, psychologists, and therapists use a five axis diagnostic system. Axis I is reserved for mental health concerns including depression, anxiety, substance dependence, ADHD, posttraumatic stress disorder, and hundreds of others. Dissociative Identity Disorder, commonly referred to as 'multiple personalities,' is an Axis I diagnosis as well. Axis III contains any medical issues that might be relevant to treatment, such as recent illness or injury that may be contributing to psychiatric symptoms. Axis IV outlines any stressful life events relevant to treatment such as recent divorce, job loss, and death of friends or loved ones.

Now that you have been sufficiently bored to death, let's focus on the axis of interest. Axis II of the multiaxial diagnostic system is reserved for diagnosis of developmental delays (mental retardation, autism, etc.) and personality disorders. Personality disorders in no way include or indicate 'multiple personalities.' While we are on the subject, Schizophrenia and Bipolar Disorder have nothing to do with multiple personalities either. So stop saying it, and start correcting other people when they say it. It's obnoxious, ill informed, and disrespectful to people who actually have to live with those disorders.

Personality disorders are among the most stigma-tizing diagnosis in mental health. Ask anyone who has worked in the mental health field about working with a client who has a personality disorder and watch them cringe as though you had just liberally salted an open wound. Pull up a chair, as this is a question that usually takes a while to answer, since we seem to love talking exhaustively about how exhausting it is to treat this population. I anticipate that some of these feelings will be palpable in my writing.

There are a staggering number of clinicians that outright refuse to treat personality disorders, or will transfer clients if one becomes evident. Because of this, whenever I happen upon a personality disorder, I tend to gravitate toward alternative diagnosis in an effort to prevent the client from being stigmatized by clinicians in the future. These disorders are so pervasive and difficult to treat that people whose entire profession is to be nonjudgmental and supportive are often incapable of controlling their negative judgments and preconceived notions when confronted with a personality disorder. Needless to say, this is a label that you would like to avoid at all costs.

Many personality disorders exist, but for the sake of brevity, only Narcissistic Personality Disorder, Antiso-cial Personality Disorder, and Borderline Personality Disorder will be discussed. The caveat to the following explanations, examples, and tangential musings is that some of these qualities will be present in yourself or folks you know. This does not mean that you or they have a personality disorder; just like being sad does not mean you have depression. Personality disorders are horrible things to live with and prevent the person from establishing and maintaining relationships with other people in the same way that others can. It's important to keep that last bit in context while reading the rest of this chapter.

Borderline personality disorder has been a diagnosis traditionally reserved for women with a penchant for hysterics. What Borderline actually is, according to the DSM IV-TR (the aforementioned diagnostic manual for mental health professionals) is a pattern of unstable interpersonal relationships, self-image, affect, and marked impulsivity observed in an adult client. There is usually a pattern of intense and volatile interpersonal (often romantic) relationships that swing violently from extreme idealization to devaluation.

Accompanying this are frantic efforts to avoid real or perceived abandonment, grossly unstable mood, flashes of intense anger, consistently unstable self-image, and chronic feelings of emptiness. Imagine every crazed, stalker, ex-boy/girlfriend story you have ever heard. Now blend them all together into one person or relationship and you are approaching what Borderline looks like.

The hallmark of Borderline Personality Disorder is that it feels very childish. It is very much like trying to reason with a four-year-old. You are either the best thing in their life, or the source of all their pain and suffering, sometimes within minutes of each other. Dr.

Jerold Kreisman wrote a book on Borderline Personality Disorder titled *I Hate You, Don't Leave Me*, the title of which pretty well encapsulates the essence of having any kind of relationship with a person with Borderline.

Providing therapy to clients with Borderline is a delicate and challenging process, but often lacks the gratification that comes from working with other types of difficult clients. This is not to say that working with a person with Borderline cannot be gratifying, and usually proves to be an interesting experience. There is a brand new, earth shattering crisis to discuss every week, and it is difficult to prevent yourself from being swept up into the tumult that is constantly swirling around the client.

Anything can represent a crisis to a client with Borderline. One of my clients tearfully discussed having a miscarriage in one session and the death of her dog with the same level of intense emotion in the next. She only mentioned the miscarriage when I inquired about her grieving process, responding in a way that suggested that it no longer warranted discussion. She then returned to her conversation about her dog.

These clients are frequently angry with their therapist, or any other supportive person in their life that challenge their views and behaviors in an effort to increase positive decision making. Borderline clients tend to externalize their behaviors and problems more efficiently than even the purest, most concentrated products of the Self-Esteem Movement. Negative consequences, relationships, and scenarios gravitate to them in their estimation. Things happen *to* them, and are completely outside of their control. I have been cursed at by more than once while attempting to get a client with Borderline to acknowledge that, just maybe, their actions had some relationship to negative consequences.

There is a level of entitlement present in people with Borderline as well. Once they have established a relationship with a person, personal or professional, they feel entitled to as much of that person's time as they wish, whenever they wish. Even when there isn't a clock in the room, clients with Borderline regularly bring up a very new and very serious issue in the last five minutes of session in an effort to extend their allotted time. Without proper boundaries, these can become marathon sessions that end without making any real progress. Because of this, Borderline clients are the only clients I will intentionally keep in the waiting room until it is precisely time for their appointment, and will end session within minutes of their scheduled ending time.

Borderline is also notorious for being associated with suicide attempts and/or threats. This is in part due to the emptiness many of these people feel. They try desperately to fill the void with sex, drugs, shopping, gambling, relationships, and any other way that can generate external value of self. Once these things prove to be fleeting at best, suicide may or may not become a viable option.

Attention seeking is a big part of Borderline, and suicidal gestures are a very effective way to meet this need. If they cannot generate positive feelings internally, they can at least generate attention from others. Vaguely insinuating that you might want to kill yourself usually results in an outpouring of support from people listing all the reasons you should stay alive. It's a surprisingly quick and efficient way to get people to stroke your ego, even strangers will do this.

Cutting and other methods of self-mutilation go hand in hand with frequent suicidal ideation, and are especially prevalent in the Borderline population. At one point, I was providing individual therapy to two sisters (sometimes not the best idea). Both were raised by the same parents, in the same home, and attended the same schools. They were both in early adulthood and lived together in their family home. Both were cutters, but only one had Borderline Personality Disorder.

The sister with Borderline made sure to cut on her lower arms, across her wrists more often than not. It was always very obvious when she had been cutting. The sister without a personality disorder was more likely to cut her upper arms or legs. She made efforts to keep her cutting a secret and would often express remorse or shame while processing it in session. They both cut, and would both express similar reasoning behind the cutting; however, one client was seeking out attention from her cutting, while the other was using it as a horribly mis-guided attempt to cope with ambiguous emotional pain.

Borderline clients make you tired and angry in session. A sense of impending doom lingers over their approaching appointment time. Exhaustion sets in immediately after they leave, and you hope you had the decency and foresight to leave a small window of time to decompress before your next appointment arrives, but you never have. These clients are exhausting because they are demanding, impulsive, and entitled. They require constant validation of their self-image, externalize negative consequences, and will respond with unbridled rage if you dare to question any of it too closely.

Sound familiar? Of course it does.

When people throw around the term 'sociopath' they are most often referring to Antisocial Personality Disorder. Antisocial does not mean that you don't feel like socializing. It has nothing to do with introversion or feeling too tired to go to the bar. Career criminals and serial killers have Antisocial Personality Disorder. To further define the difference, people who can truly be called Antisocial are often charismatic, well liked, and might enjoy socializing with others. So, like the multiple personalities thing, stop saying people are antisocial if they don't want to go somewhere or socialize – it makes you sound like an idiot.

Diagnostic criteria for Antisocial Personality Disorder include frequent failure to conform to laws and norms of society; deceitfulness or lying, often for personal pleasure and/or gain; impulsivity or aggressive behaviors; irresponsibility, specifically in maintaining work and/or financial obligations; and failure to show remorse for, or otherwise rationalize negative actions.

Whereas other personality disorders can only be diagnosed once a person is eighteen years old, Antisocial Personality Disorder has a precursory diagnosis for use with children called Conduct Disorder. Children with Conduct Disorder set fires, steal, kill and torture animals, and get into fights frequently. They show no remorse, have an absurdly external locus of control, and are often pathological liars.

Rates of Conduct Disorder have been rising in the past twenty years. Some researchers estimate that 10% of children meet criteria for Conduct Disorder, which is more than quintuple the prevalence of most other personality disorders. Being of the opinion that I am, the fact that this rate began rising about two decades ago is not coincidence. The non-violent symptoms of Conduct Disorder completely reek of the Self-Esteem Movement. Acknowledging that that is also very correlational thinking on my part, I am (begrudgingly) open to the idea that the mental health field began to focus more intently on childhood mental health needs in the past twenty years, which could just as easily explain observable increases for any childhood disorder in the same period.

Having provided therapy in jails for a time, I have run into numerous cases of Antisocial Personality Disorder and Conduct Disorder. One commonality among these clients is that there is a tangible coldness when discussing their actions. You can see and feel their lack of remorse when interacting with them. It's the vacant look in their eyes, or the detached way in which they outline a sequence of events. Sometimes it can be frightening when it occurs to you that you are in a small room with a murderer that could choke you to death and sleep soundly that night.

I have provided therapy to a single client outside of the penal system who met criteria for Antisocial Personality Disorder. He began treatment with me several years after finishing a prison sentence, and was proud of the more positive trajectory his life had taken since his release. He was a friendly and likeable person and fully engaged in the therapeutic process. I often looked forward to his sessions and always felt good about my work with him.

Several months into our treatment, he and his girlfriend got into an argument that escalated into a physical altercation. He choked her nearly to death, and told me very factually that he would have killed her had he not regained clarity at the last moment. His girlfriend called the police and he was arrested.

My client had several prior felony convictions, so if convicted, he would be sentenced as a 'habitual felon' or 'the bitch' as convicts endearingly call it. He was initially offered a plea bargain that guaranteed he would stay out of prison. Instead of taking the plea, he opted to go to trial and defend his innocence, which is where this scenario becomes truly indicative of antisocial behavior. He *believed* he was innocent.

As my client's trial approached, he would rarely acknowledge the events at all, and on those occasions, would usually justify it in such a way that his girlfriend was at fault. No amount of redirection could convince him otherwise. To ensure that everyone believed his version of the truth, he (perhaps unconsciously) became a model citizen and boyfriend to discourage testimony that might convict him. He was ultimately found innocent and resumed his life as though nothing had occurred.

During the 1970's, Ted Bundy killed nearly three dozen people, often torturing, raping, or defiling the corpses as well. Even at his execution, he expressed no remorse. When I consider the archetype of Antisocial Personality Disorder, I always think about Bundy, and probably always will.

Despite being a serial killer, people who knew Bundy often described him as likeable, handsome, and charismatic, all of which he used to manipulate his victims. His lack of remorse is not surprising, but it is precisely what makes Bundy the perfect example of antisocial behavior. He was calm, measured, and detached when discussing his victims and murders. He was not capable of empathizing with his victims or their families. It's not that he didn't care, he *couldn't* care. This inability to care or show empathy is the cornerstone of Antisocial Personality Disorder. Many people will defy rules, lie, cheat, steal, hurt people, or many other things for their personal gain, but people with Antisocial Personality Disorder lack the ability to understand how their actions affect others.

Within the realm of discussion about self-esteem, Antisocial Personality Disorder is mostly relevant due to the features of Conduct Disorder that are becoming increasing evident in society as a whole, especially in those of us born since 1980. The lingering effects of this may very well result in a higher incidence of antisocial behavior. We probably won't all become serial killers, but the cultural norms that have been put in place by the Self-Esteem Movement have discouraged empathy.

I believe that the products of the Self-Esteem Movement violate the rules and norms of society with regularity. Unfortunately for my argument and society in general, this may no longer be true. If the norms of our culture are in agreement with this behavior, then I suppose acting in accordance with these norms is no longer antisocial behavior, which is a depressing realization.

And now, dearest of readers, we arrive at the pinnacle of the argument of personality disorders and their resemblance to inappropriately high self-esteem, Narcissistic Personality Disorder. Holy shit, the children of the snowflake exhibit signs of every single symptom of Narcissism. DSM criteria for diagnosis of Narcissistic Personality Disorder include having a grandiose sense of importance and expecting to be regarded as superior; preoccupation with fantasies of unlimited success, or power; believing that they are special and/or unique and can only be understood by others who are of the same caliber of specialness; requires and demands excessive admiration; a sense of entitlement, and expectations of favorable treatment and immediate compliance to their demands; interpersonally exploitative for their own gains; lacking empathy; and often envious of others or believes that others are envious of them.

A person must show five of these symptoms in order to receive a diagnosis of Narcissistic Personality Disorder. Prevalence of this disorder in the general population is estimated at less than 1%, but I'd be willing to bet dollars to donuts that it is much, much higher than that presently. We have been conditioned by society to embody so many of these qualities that it has ruined an entire generation of people. Sadly enough, most of them are incapable of recognizing this.

Everyone loves *Breaking Bad*, and for a multitude of good reasons. The thing I love most about the series is that it made us care for and empathize with Walter White, who became one of the most narcissistic characters put on a screen of any size. Realistically, we should all have hated Walter White by the end of the show, but most of us didn't.

I was rooting for Walter like he was my hometown baseball team. I wanted him to beat the cancer, decimate his enemies, take his millions of dollars, disappear, and keep right on cooking that sweet, blue crank. But he didn't, and it made me sad. Part of me wanted him to reconcile with his family, but mostly I was in it for the drugs, money, and power. This generally positive view of Walter is something that baffled the show's creators, who intended to (and did) make a show about a good man turning evil, and had serious doubts that even giving him terminal cancer could make viewers care about him as he spiraled downward.

Walter White displays most of the symptoms of Narcissistic Personality Disorder, all of which become more evident and intense as the series progresses. He believes that he is smarter and better than everyone around him. He feels entitled to consistent praise and admiration from his colleagues, and we watch Walter become visibly agitated when he cannot demand the same praise from his family members. On multiple occasions, he comes extremely close to outing himself to his DEA brother-in-law just to bask in momentary praise of his criminal mastermind.

Money was Walter's primary ambition, and he spent much of his time fantasizing about it in constantly increasing amounts, at first to provide for his family after his imminent death. Each time he meets this total, or loses his stash in some mishap, that total grows. Money became a measure of his self-worth, and since he felt extremely important, only an obscene amount of money could begin to convey that.

Walt feels special and misunderstood by others. During the show we see him briefly consider others his equal, but this dissolves as his grandiosity expands, ever outward. Because of his exponentially growing ego, he has little difficulty manipulating the people closest to him to achieve his own goals. When these manipulations involve hurting, poisoning, or murdering people, Walt quickly and cleanly justifies his actions. There are times when we see him expressing remorse, or empathizing with others, but this is all in an effort to further bend a situation to his will. He will get what he wants, at any cost, because he is special and deserves it.

Heisenberg, Walter's criminal alter ego, is even more evidence of his narcissism. Prior to fully embracing villainy, Heisenberg allowed Walter to compartmentalize his negative actions and continue to consider himself a good person. He used the name to garner the praise of his associates and enemies. He used it to feel powerful. Primarily, though, he used it to protect himself from the truth – that he was a criminal and a murderer. He used it to maintain his feelings of grandiosity as both a dying martyr, racing death to provide for his family, and a criminal mastermind who was unparalleled in intelligence, ruthlessness, cunning, and chemistry.

As his ego grows to become the only aspect of his personality, jealousy consumes Walter. He is jealous of his son's preference for his mother and uncle. He is jealous when Jesse becomes close with Mike and Gus. He is jealous when Gale is given credit for his work. He is jealous of the lavish lifestyle that his former partners are able to afford. Despite the abundant evidence of insecurity, Walter consistently assumes that everyone is jealous of him and his empire building abilities.

Walter White is one of the worst people cast as a main character in the history of television, but we were collectively on his side for the duration, no matter how ruthless and narcissistic he became. This isn't exactly out of the ordinary. Tony Soprano, Nancy Botwin, Nucky Thompson, and Dexter Morgan are all examples of horrible 'hero' characters. I wouldn't even consider them anti-heroes, they are much closer to villains, and truthfully are unlikeable, yet we remain steadfastly in their corner week after week.

As we have become more narcissistic as a culture, we increasingly identify with narcissistic characters in our entertainment. Gone are the days of the good guy in the white hat. We have no interest in that. Give us characters with ruthless ambition, who get what they want, when they want it, no matter the cost. Nobody really cares that these characters are usually the bad guys. It takes far too long for the good guys to earn enough cash to fill a storage unit, and we are no longer in the business of waiting for what we want as a society.

The snowflakes, all of whom have been hideously infected by the Self-Esteem Movement, mirror many symptoms of personality disorders. They feel entitled to more than others, without any real justification. Many feel that the rules should not apply to them in the same way as others. External validation is a requirement and should occur frequently. So should admiration, attention, and reward. I will make no effort to control my anger because it is *your* fault that I am angry, and it will be your fault if I hurt you. In fact, I don't care if my actions hurt others as long as they get me closer to what I want. Even if they wanted to care, they couldn't, since empathy is not something they were encouraged to develop.

People reared exclusively on self-esteem are impulsive and irresponsible. They have internalized the idea that they are special and unique by default, leading to exaggerated feelings of self-importance, and fueling fantasies of unprecedented power and wealth, which will certainly fall right into their unique and special laps. Special people don't accept blame, so when things go awry, it is obviously the fault of some external factor.

If this monstrous tower of self-esteem ever comes

crashing down around them, they begin to feel extraordinarily empty. The only thing they believe is that they are special. If this is no longer true, they might have to reassess the entirety of their existence. They cannot accept an existence in which they are decidedly average, so busy themselves with ignoring reality with reckless abandon in any way they know how.

The patron saint of the snowflakes is currently one Ethan Couch. Sixteen-year-old Couch is best known for not being in prison after killing four people and seriously injuring two others while driving nearly double the speed limit and under the influence of alcohol and benzodiazepines. Couch stole the beer he was drinking that evening, but that hardly seems worth mentioning.

Three hours after the accident took place, he had a blood alcohol concentration of 0.24. Playing fast and loose with the idea that the human body metabolizes alcohol at approximately .02 per hour means that his BAC was probably closer to a 0.3 at the time of the accident, which doesn't even begin to take the Valium into account. Having done some personal research on that combination of substances in my younger days, I can tell you with scientific certainty that it will knock you flat on your ass each and every time.

Couch's parents provided him with the best legal defense that money could buy, and his attorney argued successfully that Couch's life of privilege prevented him from understanding that his actions were related to consequences. Affluenza, they called it. I would be remiss to neglect the attorney's very valid argument that Couch was in desperate need of therapy, and it would be much more beneficial for him than prison. I agree with this completely, but his argument is really dividing by zero – if wealth has prevented him from understanding that his actions have consequences, perhaps experiencing some consequences may help him begin to grasp this concept.

Couch was sentenced to a decade of probation and one year in an inpatient rehabilitation center. However, no ordinary, middle class rehab would do for young Ethan. The chosen facility was a luxury rehab/resort/spa in Southern California, the kind of place you imagine actors seek out after one too many altercations with the judicial system. His parents volunteered to cover the cost of his treatment, at approximately $450,000.00, which is quite literally the least they could do.

Adolescents do stupid things with horrifying frequency. All of us are invincible as teens, and lack the judgment that accompanies having a fully developed prefrontal cortex, meaning that some leniency is in order for normal teenage shenanigans. This was not one of those times.

This wasn't even Couch's first incident with drinking, driving, and the legal system. Just four months earlier, Ethan, who was 15 at the time, was found drunk, passed out behind the wheel. He pled no contest and was sentenced to probation, community service, and an alcohol awareness class, which was a totally appropriate sentencing. He was being a reckless teenager, and granted some degree of leniency because of that. What I take issue with is the fact that he was still on probation for a prior alcohol charge when he killed several people in a drunk driving accident, and that was somehow not taken into account in his sentencing. He should have at least had to serve his probation violation sentence before going off to his treatment facility.

The Ethan Couch Affluenza defense is built upon the idea that ignorance is better than responsibility and decency. Because his choices do not directly relate to consequences, Couch is presumably able to maintain his level of self-esteem. This aggressive externalization contributes to his inability to show a shred of remorse for his actions, because it allows him to believe that his abysmal decision making had no bearing on the outcome.

If there were an award for highest achievement in the Self-Esteem Movement, Ethan Couch would be a top contender. It baffles me that we continue to uphold and reinforce a value set that consistently results in creatures like Couch, hollow, self-centered people who exhibit many symptoms of personality disorders. I am tempted to buy a trophy for him, but choose not to simply because I don't have the expendable income to buy one for the millions of other special little snowflakes who would feel entitled to trophies as well.

PARENTAL DISCRETION

Disclaimer: As the title may or may not suggest, this chapter will involve me anecdotally outlining aspects of my own upbringing in a completely indulgent and self-righteous way. Feel free to skip ahead if you have no interest in this.

The best thing my parents did for me is reinforce the idea that I am no better and no worse than anyone else. They accomplished this in a number of different ways, all of which can be attributed to the fact that they in no way bought into the ideals of the Self-Esteem Movement. I was unable to fully appreciate this as a child and teenager, but became increasingly appreciative of my upbringing as I transitioned into adulthood. Perhaps a better way of saying this is that I became increasingly appreciative *because I could* transition into adulthood. The parenting bestowed upon me helped me to build necessary skills to become an adult instead of a perpetual adolescent.

My parents were not idealistic people. Bleak would not be an unfair way to describe my father at times. They both knew that a successful life was not handed to you. We do not come from wealth, so an easy life was far from a guarantee. They both understood the value of hard work and dedication in the long term. They understood that feeling special and being special are entirely different concepts. Starting at an early age my parents made efforts to instill in me the value of work, respect, and humility. It was this unrelenting counterpoint to the Self-Esteem Movement to which I attribute many of my positive qualities as an adult.

My father, and namesake, was born the middle of five children to the hardest working man I have ever known. His father worked tirelessly to provide for his family. Dad started working on the family farm at an early age, and made to earn essentially everything he ever owned. He was a sickly kid, but quickly outgrew this and became an avid outdoorsman. He was an excellent marksman, adept at killing and field dressing most animals indigenous to the Carolinas.

Everyone's dad seems to be able to fix anything, but this is something that was actually true of my father. He was extremely mechanically intelligent and over the course of my youth, I looked on while he was rewiring houses, welding, disassembling and repairing outboard boat motors and car engines, stitching his own leg shut, and repairing and building his own firearms. He only stopped reloading ammunition after literally blowing his eye out of its socket, and miraculously retaining use of that eye. Unfortunately, I was never that mechanically inclined, and he was never that intellectual, so we had little in common outside of shared interest in cars and driving them recklessly whenever possible.

Dad was a 'man's man' chock full of (somewhat misguided) tradition, and also grit. Lots and lots of grit. He was the type of guy you assumed could walk into the woods with a pocket knife and some matches and survive for years. Being a man of tradition, he expected his household to run according to his (antiquated) values. This was often a point of contention in our household.

For a brief time after graduating from high school, Dad lived in Raleigh, which was the only city for hundreds of miles. Aside from that, he lived his entire life living less than two miles from his childhood home, which was within the same two miles of his father's childhood homestead. His narrow frame of reference prevented us from having the most positive relationship, but his stubbornly pragmatic outlook on life helped to guide my development in a positive direction. I never got to properly express this to him before his death, which is something that I will likely regret for many years to come while I try to do the same for my own children.

My mother is the youngest of two children and grew up less than twenty miles from my father, but the environment was markedly different since she lived in an actual town instead of the sprawling rural desolation in which my father and I spent our youth. Her father was a successful and hardworking businessman, who owned and operated a sizeable garment factory. Her mother always worked, but would be better described as a career socialite. Well, as much of a socialite as one can aspire to be in a reasonably small town with very little in the way of culture.

256

Mom has always been measured in her approach to all things, including parenting. Fortunately, she had more in common with her father than her mother in that regard. She valued hard work, but also the upward mobility that is more obtainable through higher education. She was always more intellectually inclined than my father and has always enjoyed reading, learning, and teaching. Mom always encouraged my more creative pursuits and pushed me to delve deeper into subjects of interest.

Mom put her life and aspirations on hold after I was born in order to make sure that my well-being and development were her primary focus. She returned to work once I started elementary school. Once I finished high school and moved away to college, she enrolled and finished her bachelor's and master's degrees in tandem with mine, which has always made me proud. She is a fiercely independent woman and since she and my dad divorced, has always taken measures to ensure that she could maintain her quality of life on her own. I'm sure this tenacity and independence has caused its share of problems for my step-father.

Mom was very traditional in her expectations of me. She was firm but fair and always consistent, which meant I generally knew what to expect from her, even if I didn't agree with it. I could always talk to her without too much anxiety about her reaction. Because of that, my mother and I had a much closer relationship than my father and I ever did.

Both of my parents adopted traditional parenting styles, but they were different enough to balance each other out without becoming overly oppressive or authoritarian. Their upbringings were evident in their parenting, which is true for most parents. If I am a part of a generation of self-righteous, indulgent, entitled, impulsive assholes (and I am), it does not bode well for the parenting we will provide for our children.

When I was a kid, my mother never let me win a game of checkers. I have shared this story with many people over the years, many of whom have recoiled at the idea that I was not regularly allowed to win. As a result, my victories in checkers as a child were hard won and much sweeter. I had no choice but to win and lose with honesty and dignity. I learned that nothing would be given to me and success takes work. My father took a similar approach in many respects, always competing with me at slightly above my level to encourage me to work and grow.

One of the fondest memories I have of my maternal grandfather is about billiards. Most of my fondest memories of him involve billiards. He started teaching me the game as soon as I was able to hold a cue, and held me to a high standard at all times. I was taught that billiards was once a gentlemen's game, and I would learn to play it like one.

By the time I was a teenager, I fancied myself a competent pool player. One afternoon we had played several games, of which I had won a few. After breaking, I pocketed a few more balls and made some cocky remark about clearing the table before he would have the chance to lift his cue. Hubris, ladies and gentlemen. Predictably, I completely botched the next shot. He told me to put my cue away and observe, because I needed to learn something.

My grandfather, who walked with a limp due to an old war injury, proceeded to walk around the table, and without ever completely breaking stride called and made every shot, clearing the table in less than two minutes. Once he was done, he put his cue in the rack and said to me "Bud, you will never be able to shoot pool better than me. You need to learn that there is always somebody better than you are." I will never forget that.

My Nana offered a stark contrast to the rest of my familial pragmatism. Being Italian ensured that she was going to love her sons and grandsons with the most unconditional of love. She had very little issue with telling people that she favored my uncle over my mother, and preferred me to my uncle's daughters. She was never realistic with me. She showered me with praise at any and every opportunity, and told me an insane number of times that I was sure to be rich and successful no matter what I chose to do for a living. My uniqueness and value were unquestionable in her eyes.

I have no doubt that she did this unintentionally. She likely had no idea what the Self-Esteem Movement was, she was just being a Nana in the most Italian way possible. By the time I was a teenager, her praise and compliments had lost a lot of their shine. She praised *everything* I did, so it became somewhat difficult to determine when I had actually made her proud.

I loved Nana more than I loved most other people. Her behavior balanced out some of the more starkly hewn parenting I received from other members of my family. Because she was the only person in my family behaving this way, her ridiculously indulgent and unrealistic grandparenting was quite nice. Had the rest of my family behaved in a similar fashion, regardless of their intentions, I might have become jaded, confused, and a generally worse person because of it. Much like any escape, the reprieve offered by Nana was something beneficial in small doses, but would prove harmful if taken constantly.

I am an intelligent person. That is one of the things that make me special. Obviously, my parents figured this out well before I did and made sure that I didn't allow this to fester into arrogance. They held me to standards that were realistic in relation to my abilities. I was expected to make A's because I was more than capable of doing so. Until I was in high school, a B warranted some sort of consequence. I was not allowed to be lazy and take my cognitive abilities for granted. They praised me for doing well in school, but would justifiably criticize anything below my ability. I was told I was special because I was intelligent, but I was never told I was special without reason.

When I was in elementary school, all third grade students were given an IQ test, but I was in my early twenties before I ever knew my IQ score. My parents chose not to share the results of other tests as well. They simply saw no reason to give me anything to feel superior (or inferior) to other people, and I am better for it. They had no control over my cognitive abilities, but could (and did) control whether or not I was an elitist prick about it.

My parents would praise me when I exceeded their expectations, but also had no problem pointing out areas in which I underperformed. My father was especially quick to identify areas in which I was worse than most other people when I appeared to be getting too big for my proverbial britches. As was exhaustively mentioned at the beginning of this book, I was generally awful at baseball. My parents would tell me very factually that I would probably play more than two innings per game if I spent more time practicing. It's not that they were being mean or unloving, they were just being realistic with me. Had I spent time practicing baseball instead of whatever I was doing instead, I probably would have become a better baseball player. Mom and Dad made sure that situations were presented in such a way that I was responsible for my own choices, actions, and consequences. Without knowing it, they were reinforcing the concept of having an internal locus of control, which allowed me to assume ownership of my successes and my failures as I grew.

Another positive thing my father did for me, which I never fully appreciated while he was among the living, was regularly making me do things I wasn't particularly good at doing. Splitting firewood was the bane of my existence as a kid. I was a small and clumsy child; swinging an axe at logs was never a particularly safe or successful endeavor for me. By forcing me into situations that would frustrate me, I was able to observe that every person has their own differing talents and skill sets. This taught me to appreciate my strengths and acknowledge my weaknesses in a realistic fashion.

At times, my dad was needlessly quick to point out things I was not good at and/or tell me that being smart didn't make me better than anyone else. On more than one occasion he pointed out that my lack of mechanical and agricultural skill would put me at a tremendous disadvantage during any sort of economic depression or apocalyptic scenario. It's worth noting that when my dad thought about the apocalypse, he was almost certainly thinking about *The Postman*. While this was paranoid, unnecessary, and a little bit mean spirited on his part, it kept me realistic and humble, which are qualities that have come in handy as an adult. Basically, the best thing my father ever did for me was to remind me that I was just another regular jackoff, I just happened to be a bit smarter than most of the other regular jackoffs.

I was allowed to fail as a child, and made to learn from my mistakes. My mother was, and continues to be, a firm believer in natural consequences. Her favorite expression when I was a teenager was "I've given you enough rope to hang yourself; it's up to you what you do with it." She would allow me more and more freedom of choice as I earned it, but would also stand aside when she saw the warning signs of impending doom on the horizon. I honestly have no idea how many times she knew I was lying to her, or making an obviously terrible choice about something.

Mom knew something that the proponents of the

Self-Esteem Movement did not – allowing your child to experience the natural (often negative) consequences of their decision making is a learning tool. Had she protected me from my poor choices, I may not have learned how much my choices impact my life. I'm sure it hurt her to see me suffer the negative consequences of my actions, but she stood steadfast. She knew that the pain would fade in time, but the lessons I gleaned from them would be lasting.

My parents gave exactly zero shits about what anybody else was given or allowed to do. It was not their concern if someone got a new car, what time curfew was for my peers, who got to go on spring break, or who didn't have to get a job. They developed their parenting style and stayed true to it. It was not without faults, but the consistency was admirable in any case.

I was required to work, and expected to buy many of the more frivolous things teenage boys are inclined to buy. My parents encouraged me to save money, and incentivized this by agreeing to match my savings to help me buy a car. They discussed responsible money management and budgeting with me, and I had to maintain my own insurance coverage in order to continue driving. There was no better way to motivate me to manage my money appropriately than tying it directly to my ability to move freely about the rural wasteland from which I hail. My parents ensured that I had no false perceptions about the value of work or money, and they did this by refusing to be overly indulgent despite the changing norms of our society.

One of the last real lessons of my childhood came during the summer before I moved away to college. My dad sat down with me one day shortly after I had turned eighteen, and in a very matter of fact way said something to the extent of "Son, you're grown now. Soon you will move away to go to school and start your life. This will always be your home, but once you leave, you will never live here again. You're smart and can be successful, so go out and make a good life for yourself." Age was enough to constitute adulthood in my father's traditional value set. I was old enough to vote, fight, smoke, and buy pornography, so I was also old enough to deviate from the path I had walked with my parents.

This was terrifying at the time, but always acted as a semi-present motivator for me as I became an adult in more than age alone. His last act of transitioning me from childhood to adulthood was to set his expectations, encourage me, and remove my safety net. Swim or drown. Looking back as an adult, I know that my parents would have allowed me to move back home had I needed to. At the time, it felt like I had no choice but to succeed, so I conducted myself as if success was my only option.

Make no mistake, it was not all sunshine and rainbows in the Willis household. My parents and their chosen parenting style were not without shortcomings. Having only attended mass a few times in my life, I can safely say that I am weighed down by just as much Catholic Guilt as most actual Irish Catholics due to my mother's preference for being 'disappointed' instead of 'mad.' It took me much effort and discomfort to learn how to assertively communicate during a conflict, as this was something that I was never encouraged to do. My father liked to yell and he didn't like to hear anything in response. This is something I continue to struggle with – the more intense the conflict, the more likely I am to retreat inward and wait for the storm to pass. The rules of my childhood home were consistent, but needlessly strict in some instances. Looking back, though, none of this really matters within the larger context of my life. These complaints pale in comparison to the positive aspects of the parenting I received.

We all bear the scars of our upbringing, but not all of us are so effectively prepared to face the harsh realities of adulthood. My parents accomplished this by refusing to take the easy road and invest in the short term gratification of the Self-Esteem Movement. I can say with confidence that my parent's refusal to foster baseless self-esteem in me has made me a better adult than I otherwise would have been. And for that, I am forever grateful.

DELPHIC WISDOM

I have spent the entirety of this book dissecting the downfalls, failures, and overall shortsightedness of the Self-Esteem Movement. Since criticism is markedly easier to do than most things, and only slightly more difficult than doing nothing at all, I was never going to allow myself to merely criticize without also attempting to offer some solutions. These are not tremendously well thought out, but will at least offer some talking points to build upon. If I had a definitive solution to our cultural ills, this would have been a much different book from the start. This effectively serves as your warning to take the following with a sizeable grain of salt.

Three proverbs adorn Apollo's temple at Delphi. The two that are best known translate into English as 'know thyself' and 'nothing in excess.' I have always felt that these are sound advice for almost anyone no matter their current circumstances. As a therapist, my entire career is based on gaining a better understanding of self. We cannot understand anything unless we understand ourselves. I work with clients to find a more balanced and congruent existence, which usually leads to a happier daily life. Too much of anything (especially good things) is always detrimental. In my experience, both personally and professionally, self-awareness and moderation are the keys to a balanced and satisfying life.

An excess of self-esteem has, and will continue to generate individuals who have a diminished ability to empathize with others, feel entitled to success and happiness, and have a blinding need to be considered special by any and everyone. We have moved past casual use of self-esteem as a culture and have indulged with a level of excess typically associated with Keith Richards. If self-esteem were a drug, your children would have already stolen and pawned your television for another hit.

By indoctrinating children with the idea that only the highest self-esteem is acceptable, we are not effectively teaching moderation and balance. We are encouraging excess. Being an adult *requires* balance. You must balance your career with your home life, and your family life against your social life. Having too much of any of these never results in a happy person. Adults are usually aware of this reality, which means that we should understand how important it is to teach children the value of moderation and balance.

In his work on the concept of villainy, Chuck Klosterman asserts that a villain is a person who knows the most, but cares the least. In this instance, adults understand the importance of moderation and balance, yet, because of the Self-Esteem Movement do nothing with this knowledge, showing that they also care the least. We have stopped caring about what happens to children once they reach adulthood.

Don't be a villain.

Teach children the value of moderation by allowing them to balance winning and losing. Victory is much sweeter when paired with the bitterness of defeat. Let them experience sadness, and help them to feel happy again. Not only does this teach effective coping skills, it also teaches the value in simple feelings of happiness.

Help your children succeed without manufacturing success for them. Stand aside and allow them to fall short and learn about failure while they are still in a safe environment. Reinforce the idea of learning from failure and teach them how to balance their expectations and outcomes. Sometimes our expectations are unrealistic, but it is infinitely harder to learn how to make realistic goals as an adult than it is as a child.

Parents who consistently intervene to guarantee favorable outcomes for their children are creating adults who feel entitled to success. This outcome should not be surprising. If something has happened in a particular way for literally all of my life, of course I will expect it to continue happening, and rail against circumstances that challenge this consistency. Humans are, and will forever be, creatures of habit.

Show your children that perception and reality can be very different things. You can teach your kids how to approach things in a realistic fashion without being mean spirited. Just be honest with them. Presenting information in a realistic way encourages children to adopt a more pragmatic approach to their own lives. The positive is balanced by negative. Without sad, we would not be able to appropriately contextualize happy. There is no success without failure. If all we are fed is candy and chocolate, we cannot be expected to know that sweet is preferable to bitter.

A universal observation about the parenting of the Self-Esteem Movement is that it is needlessly selfish in the name of fostering positive emotions. This seems to be the result of the shortsighted idea that protecting children from pain will help to foster self-esteem and a positive self-concept. The thinking behind this was likely that adults with high self-esteem would be somehow impervious to pain. I think enough time has passed that we can all agree that this is a very untrue statement.

Children of the Self-Esteem Movement are at a diminished ability to cope with negative outcomes as adults because they were not allowed to experience pain as children. The solution is evident in the problem here – allow your children to be hurt by failure, and teach them how to effectively cope with it. Being a child is about learning in a safe environment. Parents are responsible for teaching their children the necessary skills they need to become successful as an adult. This is true for almost all mammals. Coping with pain and negativity is a necessary skill for adult humans.

Children who experience some emotional pain and are helped to understand it, learn from it, and effectively cope with it will almost certainly become more resilient and well-adjusted adults. Those who never developed appropriate coping skills cannot successfully navigate many of the negative situations that adulthood will present them. Every parent wants the best for their child.

Doing this properly means thinking long term and being prepared work much harder than easy and indulgent parenting styles would have you believe you should.

Failure is not an exclusively negative experience. There is much learning to be had from failed attempts. We learn about ourselves and increase our mastery over whatever we just attempted. Overpraising children discourages the growth and learning that accompany failure. It generates people who require frequent praise and validation. The gross overpraise encouraged by the Self-Esteem Movement has created countless people who are terrified to attempt anything that is not certain to end in success. Without succeeding and the requisite praise that accompanies it, we may not be able to maintain our accustomed level of self-esteem. Our current values are such that achieving nothing is preferable to failure.

Accept that the television is lying to you and your children. We are not all entitled to fame. We are not all intelligent. We are not supposed to be happy at all times. We are going to (and probably should) doubt ourselves at times. Happy endings have never been guaranteed. We are not all special little snowflakes. Knowing this means that it is the responsibility of parents to offer their children balance and reason. The teachings of parents should serve as a powerful counterpoint to the lies told to our children with regularity by our televisions. Children model the behavior of their parents. If you yell when you get angry, your children probably will too. If you refuse to buy into the pandering bullshit on your television, chances are they will follow suit.

For the love of any and everything you hold to be holy, be specific when telling a child they are special. There has never, and will never be a person who is special in all aspects of their being. Jesus of Nazareth might have been a terrible carpenter. Facets of our existence that make us special are to be treasured. These are the things that we can do objectively better than most other people, and raise our self-esteem in healthy and realistic ways. By telling children they are vaguely special ad nauseam, we dilute the positive impact of the things that actually make them special.

Everyone deserves to know that they are special, regardless of their age. More than that, though, everyone deserves to know *why* they are special. It is easy to arbitrarily state that a child is special, but it only takes slightly more effort to point out something that actually is special about them. This is the difference between authentic and lasting self-esteem, and the cheapened, over inflated self-esteem currently peddled. Realistically, it has become an issue of quality or quantity. Rational people choose quality more often than not.

Every child is special in the eyes of their parents. From an evolutionary standpoint, this is an instinct developed by humans to ensure that they protected and cared for their offspring long enough for them to survive and have offspring of their own. Be mindful that just because your child is special *to you* doesn't make them special to everyone else.

I honestly believe that my daughter is the prettiest baby in the world. I think she is an incredibly special human being. I am also cognizant of the fact that there is presently nothing that would make her special to anyone other than my friends and family. To the outside world, she is just about as unspecial as it gets. To my wife and me, she is the single greatest thing that has happened in the history of events. Both of these statements are simultaneously true for most babies, and it is the duty of parents to integrate and balance both of these truths for themselves and their children.

As a parent, you need to be honest with yourself. It is okay to think your child is amazing and special, but you owe it to your child to prepare them for a world that does not share your enthusiasm. I want my daughter to know that she is special and to value those aspects of her person. I want her to be self-aware and have a good self-concept because I don't want her to be easily taken advantage of. More than that, I want my daughter to be prepared for what adult life actually entails so she is not crippled and broken by reality.

Reinforce positive qualities in your children. Teach them that success is not a guarantee and takes work. Start small – have them work toward a toy they want, or dinner at their favorite rodent themed pizza establishment. Rewarding this behavior encourages development of a stronger, more consistent work ethic. It teaches children that we work for success and rewards as adults instead of waiting around for them to be given to us. Hopefully they internalize these lessons and strive toward earning things instead of assuming these things are owed to them.

272

THE SNOWFLAKE EFFECT

The style of parenting encouraged by the Self-Esteem Movement has backfired, resulting in entirely new kinds of parental neurosis. Parents have become extremely anxious due to feeling societal pressure to produce *perfect* children. If these kids aren't completely without fault; if they are not intelligent, talented, diverse, socially astute little adults, then you have completely failed as a parent. Good is no longer good enough.

The Self-Esteem Movement has created the expectation that children are special, unique, and will be successful and happy at all times. By internalizing these values, parents now assume that this should be true of their children. Because children are no longer to be blamed for things, they must be at fault if their child does not live up to these impossible standards.

Not only are we now expected to be perfect and have perfect children, parents are expected to provide the highest quality of life for our children. That quality has very little to do with quality and everything to do with consumer goods and other expensive trinkets that we must provide, lest we be accused of being neglectful. In order to provide in this way, while still managing to pay the mortgage, car payments, student loans, and credit card bills, the vast majority of homes require two incomes. This peppers in guilt to compliment the complex and robust flavors of angst, because it is no longer feasible to have one parent spending the majority of their time nurturing our children. Once we allow this guilt to creep in, it efficiently decimates the spirit of even the most competent parents.

Now we arrive at the only piece of advice directed at the parents desperately struggling to keep their unique their little snowflakes from melting. Your kids are not perfect, nor should they be. Get to know this fact. Embrace it. Love it. It is your salvation.

Freeing ourselves of the Self-Esteem Movement will not only have an immeasurably positive impact on children, but also reduce the anxiety that is prevalent in modern parenting. Once you aren't perseverating over every aspect of your performance, you might actually enjoy the act of parenting. The less you worry about making perfect and infinitely happy children, the happier your children (and entire family) will be. To move forward, we must go back.

Many feel that a return to tradition is in order. Traditional parenting did not foster entitlement and create a generation of people who have floundered through early adulthood, hopelessly under prepared for the challenges of independence. However, it *did* create the generation of people responsible for creating the Self-Esteem Movement and style of parenting that has culminated in a generation of special little snowflakes. Here again, is a case for moderation. Perhaps we should take a moment to consider becoming less indulgent without swinging back into an excessively stern and strident kind of parenting. Moderation is the only thing that can prevent the pendulum from swinging past reason time and again.

EPILOGUE

For thirty years, the snows have tumbled end-lessly downward. Rays of sunlight and warmth are finally burning through the clouds. The drifts are slowly beginning to melt away. Those not frozen begin to dig. Outward and upward, hungry for freedom. Longing for the taste of fresh air and the warmth of the sun on their face. Desperately, they inch forward.

For decades they have been trapped in a still, white hell, crushed under the weight of a million special snowflakes. Silently they have been waiting for the snows to melt and the storms to blow over. We have waited long enough. Waiting has done nothing. It will take much effort to free ourselves from the snows that have imprisoned us.

As the snow softened, those who had grown weary of waiting seized the opportunity to reclaim their free-dom. Squinting, they stepped into the sunlight for the first time in many years, blinding them as they survey their surroundings. Snow still covers everything, but others are beginning to break through the surface. Some busy themselves digging out fellow survivors while others look to the sky. The storms are finally subsiding

With any luck, those who have dragged themselves

from the snows will begin to excavate what remains of our pre-snowflake culture. Soon enough, a soggy baseball diamond becomes visible. Once it has dried and the baselines have been freshly laid, maybe that baseball game will begin again. Hopefully we have the good sense to turn on the scoreboard this time.

The Self-Esteem Movement has consistently proven to be a failure. Despite this, we cling to the idea that the most important thing we can do for a child is to manufacture high self-esteem in any way possible. Not unlike the actual manufacturing industry, the positive feelings we are presently building for children is of abysmally low quality. It takes far too much time to hand craft individuality and self-worth, so we attempted to mass-produce it.

Because the values of the Self-Esteem Movement have been a part of our cultural zeitgeist for so long, we have deeply internalized them. This is not a problem that will go away on its own. Like a cancerous tumor, neglect will only foster growth. Action is necessary. If we do not change now, we risk losing our window of opportunity to properly rectify our value system and will be forever lost in the blizzard of self-esteem.

If you have made it this far, I sincerely thank you. It is my hope that this has been more than the inane and fragmented ramblings of yet another product of the Self-Esteem Movement. A person who thinks he is in some way special and unique because his values are steeped in tradition, making them subjectively better than the values typically held by his generation. Someone with such a blindingly unique perspective that he has written a cultural criticism of his own generation while maintaining a largely outside perspective.

When I began writing this book, I was sure I had been unaffected by the Self-Esteem Movement. I was not a snowflake, fluttering about in search of validation. I have never felt entitled to success, but have undeniable difficulty coping with failure. I have always cowered behind my cynicism. I don't think I am better than anyone, let alone everyone. I knew all of this, yet, when I started writing, I was certain that I was special, and better than most of my generational cohort because of my intrinsic value system. Now that I have reached the end, I am no longer so certain of this truth. Maybe I'm not special after all. Maybe I'm another snowflake, just like the rest.

Now get off my fucking lawn you scumbag kids.

ABOUT THE AUTHOR

Trey Willis isn't his name at all, but not in that fancy pen name sort of way. His given name is Lionel Elbert Willis III, but he has never been called that by anyone who actually knew him. He was born and raised in rural North Carolina and unapologetically loves his home state. He has been in an embarrassing number of arguments with Ohioans about the Wright Brothers, at least one of which took place in The Smithsonian.

Trey earned his bachelor's degree in psychology from the University of North Carolina at Wilmington, and master's degree in counseling from the University of North Carolina at Charlotte. His education in sarcasm hails from Parts Unknown, much like The Ultimate Warrior. His rampant cynicism is entirely self-inflicted. He is a practicing therapist and occasionally an adjunct psychology professor. Now he fancies himself an author.

Trey lives in Wilmington, North Carolina with his wife and daughter. He also has two dogs and a cat, but finds that he is much less fond of them now that he has a child.

CPSIA information can be obtained at www.ICGtesting.com
Printed in the USA
LVOW11s1719170415

435054LV00004B/154/P

9 781499 795424